METRO

METRO

SIN CITY CHRONICLES

MARK RUSIN

Disclaimer: *The story you are about to read is true to the best of my recollection. Some of the names and locations have been changed to protect the guilty!*

Loop O Press
Chicago, Illinois

ISBN Print Book: 978-0-578-80093-6
ISBN ebook: 978-0-578-80412-5

Book Designer: Christy Collins, Constellation Book Services

Printed in the United States of America

MATTY MATTERS!

This book is dedicated to the wonderful and happy memory of Matthew Beuke from Hinsdale, Illinois. "Matty," as he was known to his family and friends was an amazing young man and inspiration to us all. He battled Lou Gehrig's disease (ALS) like a true warrior during the last few years of his life. I had the honor of being "Uncle Marky" to Matty and I know he is watching down on us now from the heavens. Matty was only thirty years old when our good Lord brought him home to eternal life. We all love and miss you Matty.

Uncle Marky and Matty—September, 2019

It is also dedicated to all first responders who have died in the line of duty. It is their dedication to their oath that we should never forget. God bless those who selflessly rush to danger and put their lives on the line for complete strangers. They are all heroes.

Contents

METRO

One small word that strikes fear into the hearts of every Las Vegas criminal. From 1980 through 1983, I was honored to serve as a uniformed police officer there in Sin City, assigned to work the fabulous Strip. There I responded to, witnessed, investigated, and was involved in some of the funniest, most unique, scariest, and saddest hair-raising experiences possible as a first responder.

The following short stories are actual and personal accounts which I lived through from the time before and after I left Chicago in 1980, until I resigned from the Las Vegas METRO Police Department in 1983 for "greener pastures" and a Federal badge with ATF.

These stories will give you some understanding of what goes on in a day of the life of a white kid from Chicago and then Las Vegas copper. It was during the time when Chicago mobsters allegedly ran Sin City and there was no such thing as a "hate crime". These stories will make you laugh, squirm, and probably cry. It did just that when I lived through them, and later when I wrote about them.

I must admit that as a young, single, in shape, and rather handsome (with all my hair back then) fun loving all-American male, I thoroughly enjoyed every minute of the police ride and hope you do, too. I mostly enjoyed the true camaraderie and fraternal love only cops have for one another. I sure do miss those guys.

Trust me, all cops are heroes. Who else do you know that will take an oath and put their lives on the line for a stranger, knowing they could kill or be killed by another stranger? When everyone else runs away from problems and dangerous situations, cops run to them. It's just what we do. We don't ask for much in return, but a little kindness and respect would be nice. God knows we've earned it. Now please just sit back and enjoy the ride...

The Beginning: The Tough Streets of Chicago

It was an early summer night on the south side and I was out "collecting" from my Sun-Times and Tribune paper routes. As I came around the corner of a three story apartment building, a black guy grabbed me from behind and his Mexican buddy came at me with a knife from between the parked cars. It was the first pump of adrenaline I had ever felt in my eleven-year-old body. I had 73 hard-earned dollars in my pocket and I was damned if these two punks were gonna take them!

I kicked the fat Mexican in his left shin so hard that his knife fell to the ground. I immediately turned on his skinny black accomplice with all the rage and fury I could muster. My fists were flying. Breaking loose, I ran faster than a cheetah through the prairie between apartment buildings, actually amazing myself at how fast I could run. Funny how quick you can be when your fear is off the charts.

Into the next three story apartment building and down the stairs I raced, with the two now-pissed-off robbers in hot pursuit. I put my shoulder into a door that had a security chain on it as I saw the knife thrown at me hit the concrete wall with a spark. I knew the old blind lady who lived there. "Mrs. Braun, it's me, Mark, your paperboy, and I am being robbed," I huffed as I slammed the door. In a quick frenzy I then slid her chairs and couch in front of the door as a quick barricade and asked to use her phone.

It was 1966, and I was just a couple of short city blocks from my home. It was obvious that these guys were watching me. As I waited for Chicago's finest to respond, Mrs. Braun calmed down and got me some cold water. She and her husband had been customers on my paper route for some time and she was a nice older lady. All I could think was that my only witness to this attempted robbery was blind...Beautiful!

The copper showed up in about 10 minutes and he picked the knife up off the basement floor just outside Mrs. Braun's door, looking at where it had chipped the bricks. It was a rather large folding knife with a 6-inch blade that he would take to have fingerprinted, so he said.

Then he scolded me, "Kid, you could have got killed by these animals!"

Here I was all proud of myself to have averted the robbery, but in all fairness, the cop was right. Getting stabbed for 73 bucks is generally pretty stupid. I explained that I did a lot of wrestling with my Dad and I had had a few scrapes in the neighborhood while growing up, and especially while playing hockey. I thought I could handle the two strangers who were definitely not from our neighborhood. That and, I guess, even at that early age I was a hard headed Polack who wasn't going to let these two punks relieve me of my hard earned cash! To make the officer feel better I agreed it was pretty stupid, but only because of the knife!

We then got into his squad car and drove around the neighborhood looking for the two who we both knew were long gone. I must admit that back then I watched a lot of Adam 12, Dragnet, and other cop shows, and I felt pretty good in the old blue and white marked unit. We drove past Vittum Park, where some of my buddies saw me and wondered what the heck was going on. I felt pretty cool. It was actually my first squad car ride and I was hooked. I was just happy to be in the front seat and not handcuffed in the back!

When we drove up to my house my Dad was out front watering the flowers, and I will never forget the look on his face as he dropped the hose. He was somewhat perplexed, and rightly so. He landed somewhere between wanting to kick my little ass for the bad thing he figured I had done and hugging me because I was a victim of a knife wielding attack and still in one piece. It was a priceless moment.

The officer was cool and explained what a brave kid I was. My Dad was proud of me and put his arm around me. He then thanked the officer and waited for him to leave. As the copper turned on South 50th Street and out of sight, my Dad looked at me and said, "Let's go!" We both ran to his Rambler station wagon to go look some more for those two punks (who messed with my Dad's son).

Needless to say, our search ended to no avail. I played it up pretty good and got my Dad to stop at McDonald's to buy me a vanilla shake. I was also thinking of a hot dog from Jack's cart at Archer Avenue and La Porte, but left that thought for another time.

And from that day on I always wanted to be a cop!

Stories from the South Side

The south side of Chicago is quite a place. Having been born and raised there, I quickly learned about neighborhoods, street gangs, school districts, and last but not least, Catholic Church parishes. I grew up near the busy intersection of Archer and Cicero Avenues, just five city blocks north of Midway Airport. It was in the Our Lady of the Snows Catholic parish where I attended grammar school, and was proud to be just one of the kids from the neighborhood of Vittum Park.

As a kid, we played baseball, basketball, lineball, fast pitching or strike-out, football, softball, and ice hockey all year round at the park. That is where I learned to skate when I was only six years old. That is also where I learned to fight. As kids, we would get into scuffles every now and then. Learning to fight and to hold your own was important in a place where competition was so high.

Growing up with two loving parents as the fourth kid in a family of five, I hold some of the fondest memories I could have ever asked for. The farthest back I can remember is the early 60s, when hot dogs were just a quarter, phone calls were only a dime, and names like Hull, Mikita, Butkus, Aparicio, Banks, Williams, Santo, and Sayers were worshipped in Chicago by both young and old. Those were our role models. Those were our idols. Life was good back then. I loved our neighborhood and all of my friends. Those were the good old days!

In our household at 4950 S. Lamon, also known as Dick and Del's place, it seemed like sports took center stage. My two older sisters, Marsha and Cindy, attended Queen of Peace High School and their world revolved around their studies and who they were dating from the USO that month. Marsha was always more serious about stuff than Cindy, but they were both great sisters. Then there was my older brother Cliff, and then me. My little sister Sheila came along eight years later after we lost our little sister Mary at birth. That was a traumatic event, as she was stillborn and never had a chance. I will never forget the little casket that she was buried in.

One summer day when Sheila was about three or four, we were playing on the concrete front porch when she stumbled and fell down the stairs. It seemed like slow motion as I tried to catch her, but couldn't. It took three stitches to sew up her top lip. To this day I still feel bad and wish I could have caught her! Sorry, Sheila.

My older brother Cliff and I were all about sports, starting in the little league and continuing through high school and college.

As I think back to my childhood, it blows my mind that my parents, who were married for 63 years until the day they died, did so much with so little. My Dad was always the bread earner and my Ma was the housewife. The love, time, and attention they gave to all of us kids were amazing. Now that they are both in Heaven I miss them every day!

One fine day in the summer of 1961, I was only six and playing baseball at the park. I found a baseball mitt with the words "Ricky 5052 LaPorte" written in bold black magic marker lettering. LaPorte Avenue bordered the park and 5052 was just a block south of it, so I took a stroll to try and find this Ricky kid and return his lost glove. I didn't think twice about whom the glove might have belonged to or if I should keep it. I had been taught by my parents to return things that didn't belong to me. I was on a mission to see if I could find the rightful owner since it seemed like a pretty good glove. I was sure he was heartbroken to have lost it and if I found him I'd be his new hero!

When I got to the house an elderly lady was watering the lawn wearing a nice apron and I asked her if Ricky lived there. She smiled and nodded her head yes and then yelled "Reeeeeeeeeky." I waited patiently at the side of the house gangway as six-year-old Ricky appeared near the gate. He smiled as I tossed him his glove.

That was the start of our friendship, and we have been best friends ever since. In fact, from that day on I spent more time at Ricky's house than I did my own. It turned out that my act of kindness led to a great and everlasting friendship with Ricky and also served me well for my future. Ricky's Ma and Dad took me in like their second son, and I will forever be thankful to both Mr. and Mrs. "B" for that. To this day I love being part of their family. In fact, over the years we have stayed close and I have been truly blessed along with my wife Marcie to be part of their beautiful family. Ricky struck gold when he married Re (Babe) in the early 80's and they had three wonderful sons: PJ, Matty and (little) Ricky. Next to my wife Marcie, Re (Babe) is the most amazing woman, friend, ma and grandma on the planet. Over the years, I often think how lucky I was that I found Ricky's mitt back in 1961!

Ricky and I became inseparable and so good at sports that we would take on any kids our age in the neighborhood at any sport, any time. Hell, we would even kick the shit out of some of the older kids. Street football, lineball, fast pitchin', mumbly peg, baseball, hockey, basketball, pitching pennies, you name it. I recall when it came to team sports the kids at Vittum Park would not even play if Ricky and I were on the same team because the other team had no chance. We were that good and quite a team. Who could have known back then that Ricky would go on to law school and become a great Cook County prosecutor and now excellent defense attorney? Or that I would become a copper and big time Federal agent? We often laughed in our later years that I would try and put the scumbags in jail and Ricky would try and get them out!

I also grew up in the shadow of my older brother Cliff, who was always much bigger and stronger than me. He was two grades ahead of me and a great athlete in baseball, basketball, and soccer. The only thing I did better than him was play ice hockey; although he probably thinks he was better than me at that, as well. All I know is that I always had to try harder to measure up.

I followed Cliff to Quigley South High School on the south side, and then to Western Illinois University in Macomb, Illinois. All the while I tried hard to make a name for myself. It wasn't easy because I was always Cliff's little brother, and still am to this day.

One day, Cliff and I went to Ford City, a shopping center on South Cicero Avenue. Like a goof I stole a hockey puck. I just picked it up off the floor and put it in my pocket. When we got on the bus and started home I showed the stolen puck to Cliff. He went nuts. He had the driver stop the bus and made me get out and we crossed the street. We were going back to the scene of the crime and I was going to return the puck and tell the store manager that I was sorry for what I had done. To this day Cliff tells the story of scaring me "straight" and keeping me from being a criminal. All I can say is, "It was a tough lesson learned." Of course I begged Cliff all the way home not to rat on me to Dad or I would catch another beating.

Luckily for me, Cliff kept his mouth shut. This lesson taught me well; except for a few cases of beers at Skip's Liquors (when Cliff wasn't around), I never stole anything else. Of course we hid the beers under Ricky's back porch!

In November of 1963, I was in second grade at Our Lady of the Snows Grammar School when on one cool afternoon the Principal, Sister Alberta, came over the loudspeaker and sobbingly said, "President Kennedy is dead!"

I wasn't sure what that meant, but I vividly recall that all of the adults in the building were crying their eyes out. It was scary when they sent us all straight home. I remember walking through Vittum Park crying because I was freaked out. When I got home my poor Mom was weeping. My Dad came home from work and he was crying, too. Everybody was crying. Then it was like the world stood still for the next few days.

The following day we all gathered around the TV to get a look at the man who they said had shot and killed the President. I remember watching our black and white TV, and when Lee Harvey Oswald was walking toward the camera somebody shot and killed him! It was all so hard to understand back then. It was crazy to see it happen right before my eyes. I was only eight at the time but I had just witnessed history live!

When I was about 10, one night my Dad took us kids to the old Comiskey Park for a Friday night game. We were seated in the left field bleachers, and during batting practice one was hit over our heads and I gave chase. When I got to the ball, it was rolling down the old ramp. I picked up the ball with my right hand and, jumping for joy, turned around to get knocked on my ass and pummeled by four black kids who took the ball away from me and ran. When I came out of the tunnel looking like I saw a ghost my Dad gave chase, but it was too late. I remember him asking me if I had landed any punches. He was pissed!

When I was 10 and 11, I had a Chicago Sun-Times and Tribune paper route. I would get up at five in the morning to roll the papers and then deliver them before school. I remember one headline when eight nurses were murdered in a house on the south side. Some slimeball named Richard Speck was caught at a fleabag hotel after he slit his own wrists. "What a coward," I thought. It made front page news and I will never forget that headline. I remember wondering how anybody could do such a thing. I was happy that the cops had caught him so fast so that he couldn't do it again. Again, one for the good guys, but I couldn't stop thinking about those poor, dead nurses. Again, I wanted to be a cop!

Ricky and I were 12 or 13 when we were invited to a basement party at Marylou's house. She lived across the street from Ricky. When we arrived, there was a girl there with the biggest tits that we had ever seen. We called her Mountain Mama! Ricky and I sprang into action and devised a plan so Ricky could cop a feel. If that went well, I would go next.

The plan we came up with was brilliant! He would stand next to Mountain Mama and I would get near the light switch. When we were in position Ricky flashed me the sign. I turned off the lights and the next thing we heard was a loud scream then a big DOYNG! When the lights came back on, Mountain Mama was massaging her breasts with a look of horror on her face and Ricky was out cold on the basement floor. He had made a tactical error by forgetting about the steel poles that were in the middle of the basement holding up the structure. BUSTED! I (of course) quickly got out of the vicinity of the light switch.

I then had to go and get Ricky's Dad and help carry my friend across the street. Mr. "B" was so pissed! When Ricky came to, he looked like he had a third eye coming out of the middle of his forehead. Needless to say, this episode is what fueled young Ricky to go on to law school and then become a great prosecutor for Cook County! (-;

As kids, we spent most of our time at Vittum Park. It was great to be from the neighborhood—Our Lady of the Snows Catholic Parish, Vittum Park, Garfield Ridge, 8th Police District, 23rd Ward, Midway, South Side, Chicago, it was all the same! We played sports all day and had to be home when the street lights came on. From Pee Wee to Midget to Liberty league in baseball, my Dad coached all the kids and he loved every minute. I can honestly say that I don't think my parents ever missed a game for me or my brother Cliff. Looking back, those are some of my fondest memories of being a kid.

Growing up in Chicago and being an avid Blackhawks fan, I will never forget the roar at the old barn (Chicago Stadium) when Bobby Hull, the golden jet, would rev up his engine from behind the Hawks' net. The hair on my young arms would stand straight up. Talk about electricity in the air! I vividly remember going to the Rangers game with my dad when I was eleven when Bobby Hull shot a slapper from just inside the blue line. We were in the second balcony behind the Ranger's net and their goalie was Cesare Maniago. It was truly a sight to behold and I remember it like it was yesterday. I never heard so much noise as when the red light went on when Hull's slapper tickled the twine. It turned out to be a historic goal and his 51st that year, shattering the single season scoring record at that time. Amazing!

I went on to attend Quigley South High School at 79th and South Western Avenue where I was an eight-time varsity letter earner and all around jock; I earned three letters in baseball, another three in ice hockey, and two in soccer. However, my greatest love was always ice hockey. I even dreamed in those days of playing for my hometown Blackhawks to be like my heroes Bobby Hull and Stan Mikita.

I was also a die-hard White Sox fan who, like most good Chicago south-siders, despised the Cubs. When I was a freshman in the summer of 1969, my buddy Al won the Chicago White Sox bat boy contest and asked me if I wanted to be a "fill in" as a bat boy on weekends. Of course I said YES, and was soon making $6 a game and $10 a doubleheader. The visitors' clubhouse manager Mike took a liking to me and offered me a job in the clubhouse when I wasn't working as a bat boy on the field. When the Oakland A's came to town, I got a ball autographed by Joe DiMaggio who was their hitting coach that year. Here's that story:

I was 14 years old sitting in the visitors' dugout at the old Comiskey Park on a Friday night in September when Joe DiMaggio sat down beside me and asked, "Nice night for a game, huh kid?"

I responded, "It's a beautiful night for baseball, Mr. DiMaggio!"

That was the extent of our historic conversation. On the ride home that night I told my Dad (who was at the game and my ride) that Mr. DiMaggio had talked to me. My Dad seemed more excited than I was..."What did he say...what did he say?"

I told my Dad he said, "It's a nice night for a game, huh kid?"

My Dad opined, "You gotta get his autograph, he was the greatest!"

The next day there was a Saturday day game and my Dad didn't go, so I took the bus to work. I rode the Archer Express to 35th Street and transferred on 35th to Comiskey Park at 35th and Shields. I was playing catch before the game just in front of the visitors' dugout when Mr. DiMaggio appeared in the dugout from the clubhouse tunnel. I thought, "Now's my chance!" and said, "Hey Mr. DiMaggio, I told my Dad you talked to me last night!"

"Oh yeah, kid, what did he say?" DiMaggio asked.

"He said, YOU ARE THE GREATEST!" I replied.

Mr. DiMaggio just smiled and turned to Sal Bando, who played third for the A's, and said, "Did you hear that Sally?"

He was still beaming when I said, "My Dad said I gotta get your autograph!"

Joe said, "Flip me the ball, kid, and what's your name?"

I replied, "Mark with a K." I didn't want him to spell my name wrong.

I flipped Mr. DiMaggio the ball I had been playing catch with and he signed it, "To Mark, Best Wishes - Joe DiMaggio."

He then flipped it to Sal Bando and said, "Here Sally, sign the ball for the kid."

"Sure Joe." And Sal Bando signed it, as well, and then tossed it back to me.

When I got home that afternoon, I gave the ball to my Dad and he was in awe. The next day he went out and bought a plastic ball holder, and that ball was proudly positioned on the mantle of our fake Chicago fireplace for the next 20 years. I still have the ball to this day!

As a teenager I got "jumped" on a CTA bus by about 8 black kids who tried to "tune me up" and steal my Timex wrist watch and high school ring. They would have to cut off my finger to get my new ring, and the fight was on.

In retrospect it was really my fault, as I was daydreaming (probably looking at the girls) at the bus stop at Archer and Cicero Avenues northbound. All the black kids had to transfer from their Public School Kennedy in order to get home to the projects, known as The LeClaire Courts. Silly me, I knew all this but just wasn't paying attention. About 8 of them got on the bus and figured they would have some fun with me, "whitey". Like a dummy, I was seated in the back of the bus when I noticed how dark it had gotten all around me. They were now between me and the back door of the "green limousine" as we called the Chicago Transit Authority or CTA back in those days. I sensed trouble immediately, and then the fight was on!

Thank God the bus driver intervened or I might not have made it. During the melee, which lasted only two blocks, I was able to dive and grab the wire which was above the seats that signaled to the driver that I wanted to get off at the next stop. Truth is I ripped it down. He stopped the bus and the beating. Then he read those kids the riot act. Today they would call it a "hate crime". Back then they called it, "another day on the south side of Chicago." It's just how it was.

The rule back then was the blacks were tame when they were alone. But get three or more of them together and you got problems. Our motto was...One shine, no problem.... Two shines, still no problem... Three or more shines, run like hell!

One beautiful thing about Chicago back then, besides the civic pride of the neighborhoods, was that we all had names for every kind of ethnic heritage. It wasn't meant to be malicious or degrading; it was just the way it was. Whites were known as Honkies or Crackers; we had Shines or Niggers, Spicks or Beaners, Wops or Dagos, Kikes or Heebs, Krauts, Lugans, Micks, Chinks or Zipperheads, Japs or Slant Eyes and of course Poles or Polacks. It really didn't matter, as we were all fair game. There was no such thing as a "hate crime" back then. That was simply called being caught in the wrong neighborhood. That's why growing up back then in Chicago, you knew that you had better pay attention. It is still that way today, to a certain extent. In a way, it taught you to respect everyone because you might just get your ass kicked if you didn't.

And if any of you are offended reading this, you better not tell me you never told or laughed at a Polish joke! So yes, I have used the N word. Now please go and find a south side Chicago black person who hasn't used the N word or referred to a white person as a "Honky" or "Cracker". I dare you.

I finally left the city for the first time to attend Western Illinois University in Macomb, which was about 250 miles southwest of Chicago, where I majored in Law Enforcement Administration (LEA) and ice hockey. I minored in Psychology because I figured if I couldn't make it in the pros playing hockey, maybe I could be a copper and it would come in handy some day. As it turns out, it certainly did.

I also played on the varsity soccer team for one year and was the backup goalie. I loved all those guys on the team and Coach Mac and I had fun because I wanted to start every game and verbally showed my disappointment when I didn't get the "nod." It was all in good fun as everybody laughed at my antics. We all knew Jack (the starting goalie) was way better than me!

When I graduated from college in May of 1977, I moved back in with my parents and lived in their upstairs apartment for $75 a month. They only charged me for food and laundry, so it was a really good deal. I knew pretty well by then that my dreams of playing pro hockey were over, so I started to write letters to all of the Federal law enforcement agencies looking for employment. However, there was one small problem. Jimmy Carter, who had just been sworn in as president in January 1977, had immediately placed a freeze on all Federal hiring.

So, I spent the summer of 1977 running around Chicago looking for work. When I wasn't out of my Mom and Dad's house, I was lying on their front room couch watching WGN TV and hoping the Cubs would lose again. They usually did.

Finally, in the spring of 1978, I got a job as security director for a small bank called Chicago Savings and Loan at 63rd and S. Western Ave. It was a nice title, but no big deal for only $12,000 a year. Hell, we didn't even carry guns!

I also moonlighted as a bartender at Chesdan's Pizza on West Archer Avenue and the Driftwood Steakhouse at 43rd and S. Pulaski. Ricky's Uncle Mike owned the joint.

This I did while I was awaiting job openings for the Chicago Police Department and Chicago Fire Department. It was probably the only time in my life I wished I wasn't white, because affirmative action was in play.

Pepe's Show Lounge

I landed a bouncer job at a south side night club called Pepe's Show Lounge on West 63rd Street. It was a "mobbed up" joint owned by Joe and his older brother, Sam. I worked Friday and Saturday nights for $75 cash each night. My shift was 9 p.m. Fridays to 4 a.m. Saturdays, and 9 p.m. Saturdays to 5 a.m. Sundays. There was no drinking on the job!

Pepe's was quite a place and the bands were always good. There were also plenty of beautiful women who were regulars and, of course, some who were not.

At Pepe's, my partner's name was "Ace". I worked with Ace for three years and I never did learn his real name. I probably didn't want to know it. Ace was the best bullshit artist on the south side… PERIOD. He showed me the ropes, and we made so much money together that it was amazing. He was a maitre d', a loan shark, fence, and master schmoozer. He also claimed to have a good patronage city job. We worked together on Friday and Saturday nights, and sometimes I had so much cash from the job that I couldn't even fit it all in my pockets!

We worked a scam at the door, where we collected the $2-$5 cover charge then told the customers that choice seating costs extra, like in a Las Vegas showroom. We charged different amounts depending on the quality of the live entertainment and the color of the clientele who came through the door. The lounge was located in a white neighborhood and in those days no blacks were allowed in. That was the unwritten rule. The blacks and Mexicans who had the balls to try to get in would be asked to pay a $15-$20 cover charge. Then, when they got in, nobody would serve them. They would eventually say something and we would tell them, "Get out!" If they went quietly we would give them their money back. If not, we just kept it.

Sam, the owner's brother, would give us a sign and we would literally throw them out into the street if they didn't leave peacefully. Joe and Sam wanted the word to spread that blacks were not welcome in his place. They just didn't want any problems. The 8th District Tact guys (tactical unit) would come by and take it from there. After the pinch (arrest), they would stop by for a night cap or two. Hell, the boys in uniform would stop in and stand at the bar with a bottle of beer in their hand. Anything went in those days.

One night, we threw a guy out and he threw a garbage can lid like a Frisbee through the front window. People were diving everywhere. We chased that guy for blocks and whipped his ass when we caught him. Then, we carried him back to the club and dropped him in the broken glass to lay there until the police paddy wagon came to pick him up. We had Plexiglas installed after that.

In addition to the door scam, Ace and I had a side hustle as "brokers" to the selling of stolen goods. The guys in the neighborhood would break into the boxcar trains and steal anything they could get their hands on. I would get the word from Ace about what was for sale and then talk to every person who entered the joint. We would steer the customer to the guy at the bar who had the goods in his car trunk in the back parking lot. Depending on how good a night he had, he would "grease" Ace and me with a "broker's fee". I figured if I never touched the stolen merchandise, I was okay!

At that time in the late 70s, the things that moved best were 8-Track tapes, Norelco triple header shavers, radios and TVs. The best, though, were these little plastic gold necklaces with orange strobe lights. They took a little $1 battery and flickered in the dark. Those things cost me $2 a piece stolen, and I sold them like hotcakes for $15 each or two for $25. I made $8,000 in six months selling these stupid things during the disco craze. What a country!

I would wake up late on Sunday mornings before church and put all of my cash on the bed to sort the bills. They were mostly twenties, tens, and fives. I then stashed the money in shoes in my bedroom closet. I averaged about $500-$800 cash every weekend. Not bad for a 23 year old kid back in 1978! I was also making $1000 a month on my real day job which of course was taxable income.

Sam took a liking to me and said I needed to get a real job and quit chasing skirts and the almighty cash dollar. Deep down I knew he was right. That was the beginning of me contemplating leaving Chicago if the opportunity arose. Little did I know then that a gambling junket with my buddy Mike to Las Vegas would soon change my world forever!

Fire Department Dreams Up in Smoke

I told Sam that I wanted to be a Chicago Fireman, and he said that his brother Joe might be able to help me out. I wanted to get a job that would help me make a difference, where I could help people. And, at the time, I was bursting with energy, so this seemed like a great choice. I really wanted to be a Chicago Copper, but they weren't hiring white guys at that time. Sam told me to come and see Joe the next day around 2 p.m. "Tell Joe I'll be here and thanks a lot, Sam," I said.

The next day, I walked into the dimly-lit nightclub and Joe the owner and Joe the bartender were seated at a table drinking coffee. *Two great Dagos!* I thought to myself. They said, "Get yourself a cup and sit down here."

The place was neatly decorated, but there was little to see because the lighting had been turned down considerably. It was almost as if Joe wanted to keep all the attention to one table.

Joe started the conversation, "So, Sammy tells me you wanna be a fireman?"

"Yessir, that's right," I said.

"You live in the 23rd ward, don't you?" he asked.

"Yessir, the 8th police district," I responded.

I admit I was a little nervous because I had never even spoken to Joe the Owner before; he was the big boss. He was kind of like Mayor Daley and the Archbishop all rolled into one. When he spoke, people would just listen. He had that energy about him where whenever he would enter a room, people would stare in awe. It was like a scene from The Godfather!

He then explained, "That's good, because I have a friend who owes me a huge favor. Just go down to the 23rd ward tomorrow and see the state representative there named Don. I already made the call!"

He then put out his right hand and said, "Congratulations, you are gonna be a Chicago Fireman."

Joe the bartender also congratulated me and I downed my coffee and said, "Thanks a lot, fellas." It was as good as done!

Bribery or Extortion?

I had heard a lot about Chicago politics, but could it be this easy? In any event, I never told anyone about that meeting and the next day I showed up at the 23rd ward and asked to see the state representative named Don. The lady said, "Don is expecting you, so please just go in."

I wasn't sure about what to expect as I entered Don's office.

I stood in front of Don's desk and he never raised his head to shake my hand or even look at me. He said, "Joe sent you here with excellent references to be a fireman and I owe him a big favor. Normally it's four, but for you it's only two." I was stunned.

I said, rather sheepishly, "Two what?" as I thought to myself... Joe or Sam never said to me I'd have to "drop."

He said, "You know...two."

I said, "No sir, I don't know two...two what? Two hundred?"

He then pointed up with his thumb and said, laughing, "No, no, no...two G's...you got it... don't you?"

Totally dazed and confused I responded, "Not on me, but yeah I got it at the bank."

Don then said, "Good, go down to your bank and get two grand in twenties and put it in a white envelope and bring it back."

Without a word, I left the building.

As I drove the mile or so to my bank I kept asking myself if this was bribery or extortion. I was trying to think about my college class and the definitions of each. Or is this some kind of set up? I thought to myself, *Why would Sam and Joe set me up like this?* It made no sense to me. Besides, I really wanted that fireman job.

My head was kind of spinning as I got back into my car. I had the cash, that wasn't a problem, but I was really questioning myself. Should I be doing this in the first place or not? There were a lot of thoughts going in my head but I kept driving.

I drove about a mile to my bank, Archer Avenue Savings and Loan, and went in and asked the teller Sue (who knew me from grammar school) for two grand in twenties and to place them in a white envelope. She looked at me funny, so I said I was going to Vegas and didn't want any large bills. I thought the smaller bills would last longer. That was my BS story I had learned from Ace. Always have a story. She just looked at me with the south side "hairy eyeball".

I took the envelope and drove back down Archer Avenue to the 23rd ward and walked in. The state rep said, "Well, did you get it?" and I responded, "Yes."

"Good, then just drop it on my desk."

I did, and still without ever making eye contact with me he reached out his hand to me. "Congratulations, you will soon be a Chicago Fireman," he said.

I said "Thanks a lot, Sir"

As I walked out he said, "But you'll still have to take da test."

I said, "Yessir."

Some guilt and shame were brewing inside of me as I walked out. I knew what I had done wasn't right, but this was my first foray into this kind of thing, and I just hoped it would work out.

On April 1, 1978, I took the fireman's exam with about 35,000 other jobless individuals or "firemen wannabes". It was a brutal test. I will always remember that date because I missed my sister Cindy's wedding at the church that morning. She even understood, because the Chicago Fireman job was that good and it meant that much to me. I talked to her about my scheduling conflict and she totally understood, but it still left a void in my heart. Of course I attended the reception that night. Now that's a cool sister!

When I got the letter congratulating me because I placed 68th on the "best qualified" list. I was extremely excited but not surprised. I was going to become a Chicago Fireman and I was so happy! It's always good to know a guy who knows a guy in Chicago.

Then, one summer Sunday morning, just before the academy was to begin, I was sitting at the kitchen table with my dad sipping coffee and orange juice trying to relieve myself of a Rush Street hangover from the night before. I opened the Sun-Times and spit out my orange juice all over the table as I read the headlines... Chicago Firemen's Exam Rigged.

The headline hit me hard like a Mike Tyson punch to the head as I pretended like my orange juice went down the wrong pipe in front of my Dad. The article said someone was caught on the "inside" changing scores; the test was now void and the entire testing process was under investigation. The article also inferred political favors and pay offs, and as I read on my stomach ached more and more. I had to play it cool in front of my Dad because he didn't know about the payoff. All he knew was that I scored pretty high on the test. I guess I just wanted him to think that his kid was sharper than he ever thought.

All I could think about was being screwed out of a great job and my two grand going bye-bye!

Needless to say, I was very demoralized and things were never the same for me at Pepe's. It also taught me that things weren't always going to work out even if you pay your way for something.

So like a hard-headed, south side Chicago Polack (and probably a fool), I decided to go see the state rep again on my own and ask for my money back.

I walked into his building, and this time I was told by the same secretary that I needed an appointment and that he wouldn't see me and worse yet, he didn't even know who I was.

This really pissed me off, so I walked into his office and the prick sat there having a very bad case of amnesia and told his secretary to call the police. I left before they showed up, so that was that. Two G's down the drain.

On my drive home it dawned on me that the bastard probably thought I was "wired", as an investigation had already probably begun. I didn't look forward to seeing Sam or Joe that upcoming weekend. No sooner did I walk into Pepe's for my Friday night shift when Sam came up behind me and whispered in my ear, "Stay away from the state rep."

I said, "Sam, he's got my money."

Sam looked me right in the eye and with his stern, steely-eyed look said, "Mark, just let it go."

I immediately envisioned myself sinking to the bottom of the Chicago River wearing cement boots. So I decided to do the wise thing. I let it go.

And Don, if you are reading this you still owe me $2 grand with 42 years of interest, you crooked bastard!

Viva Las Vegas!

In late 1978, my buddy Mike, a fireman from Chicago, had just gone through a very tough divorce. He had a couple of all-expense paid tickets to Las Vegas and he asked me if I wanted to go. Seeing as I had never been to Vegas at that time, and considering the price was right, I jumped all over that deal.

We flew nonstop from Chicago to Vegas and stayed at the MGM Grand. Three days and two nights for free! Well, free my ass. I blew the first $500 I took by the end of the first day and all I had was $500 left. Vegas with all its glitter was cool, and I especially liked the beautiful women, action, and no last call.

The second day we decided to go to The Riviera Hotel and play a little blackjack. I figured what the hell, as I wanted to get back even. I really fell in love with the game, and the pretty little Italian dealer wasn't bad, either. I enjoyed just being there, and it wasn't long before I was exchanging glances with her. We flirted with each other for a while when the pit boss wasn't watching and she said she would pick me up in valet after she got off work at 2 a.m. I said I would be there waiting.

So at 2:10 a.m. that next morning I was standing at valet at "The Riv" and this white T-top Camaro came along with this hot looking driver smiling like a big dog. I was probably smiling brighter. I got in and she took me to some off the strip joint called The Starboard Tack.

Her name was Louise and we drank and ate until almost noon that day. She was a neat gal who told me that the police department there was always hiring new cops because the town was growing so fast. Me, a cop in "Sin City"? I must admit that thought intrigued me. It was something I had never considered, and my adventurous side was coming out. Besides, I figured the icing on that cake would be to get into Louise's pants!

I gave her my parent's address in Chicago and asked her to send me next weekend's employment notice from the newspaper there. She did and I admit that I was excited to see what they had to offer as a career in law enforcement.

I filled out the Las Vegas METRO police notice when it came in the mail, and also attached my rather weak resume. I also sent Louise a bouquet of red roses for a "thank you" gesture. It was all I could do at the time. I was hoping that becoming a cop in Sin City might be just the fresh start I needed.

My application was answered by some correspondence that said I would be testing in the spring of 1979, at my own expense, if I still wanted the job. I then called their employment office and said I would be there. When I told my parents about it at the supper table that night, they both said it was a waste of time. They both chimed in, "Mark, you will never leave Chicago!"

Not that they weren't supportive of my hopes and dreams, but they both knew how much I loved Chicago!

In my own mind, I was just wondering to myself, "What do I have to lose?"

I had a loving family that I knew would always take me back if things didn't work out. I wanted to be a cop and that was what I went to school for. I wanted to get a good job on my own without having to pay someone off. Louise was hot and lived in a cool condo with her little dog Keno, and I was 24 and single.

My girlfriend Lynne had just dumped me for an older guy because I was just a bum without a job. Besides, I wasn't the right color or gender for the Chicago Police force. I was probably being looked at for bribery to get the fireman's job and the Feds weren't hiring at that time, either.

Louise picked me up when I flew to Vegas and I stayed with her at her condo. We actually slept in separate rooms after she told me that her boyfriend was in prison for income tax evasion. Of course I was happy enough with a place to stay and a car to use, not to mention her Italian cooking. Her little dog Keno loved me. She was the cutest damn dog I ever saw.

I drove Louise to work at The Riv in the early morning and had to pick her up after her shift. That way I got to use her car all day long to go for the METRO police test.

The first day of testing was the physical agility part. You had to run and finish an obstacle course; crawling, running, and jumping in less than 90 seconds. If you passed, you stayed in the running. If you didn't you went home. I passed and didn't find it difficult at all because I was a jock and in pretty good shape at that time.

The next day was the second part of the test, which was a written exam which you had to score 70% or better to stay in the running. If you didn't score at least that high, you were done. I scored 76%, which was good enough as I always knew I wasn't the sharpest knife in the drawer.

Then the third part on the third day was a psychological inventory exam, which was pass or fail. It was designed to weed out all the "crazies". Don't ask me how, but I passed.

The fourth and last part on the fourth day was the oral board interview. 70% was passing again, and if you didn't score at least 70% it was all over. I scored a very weak 72%. Little did I know then that no recruit received an oral grade of more than 80%.

They then added your written score test results to your oral score test results and divided by two. Using that formula, my average score was 74% and that placed me on the applicant list to be hired pending a clean background investigation, which I also passed.

So in November 1979, I got the call at my parents' house that I would be sworn in as a Las Vegas METRO police officer on January 16, 1980, the day after my 25th birthday. I hung up the phone and started screaming with excitement. I felt great because I finally got something good on my own. It really was a new beginning.

Good Old Chicago Traffic Court

It was late December that same year in Chicago and I knew that in a few weeks I would be driving to Las Vegas to become a police officer there.

I was driving my 1978 Chrysler Cordoba when all of the sudden the blue lights of "Chicago's Finest" pulled me over on the Stevenson Expressway just a few miles from my parents' house. It was a terrible, cold rainy night and I was on my way home from partying with some friends on Rush Street.

The copper behind the steering wheel beeped his horn and motioned for me to come back to his squad car. I did, even though the pouring rain and mist from the screaming trucks flying by was no fun. The officer rolled down his window about six inches (to not get wet) and asked me if I knew how fast I was going. I said, "No," and he pointed to his radar gun blinking 74 and said, "You were going 74 in a 55."

I said I was sorry and had no idea and just wanted to get home on this terrible night. He then said, "Me and my partner here haven't eaten yet."

I immediately thought he was a crooked copper or it was a setup, as I had heard horrific stories of the traffic unit before. My new job flashed before me as I said, "I don't have any money, officer."

He said, "Good, then give me your license and go wait in your car."

When he was done writing me a ticket, the copper then beeped and motioned for me again to come to his driver's window. I was so pissed I just stayed in my car. I thought, "If you are gonna write me a ticket because I didn't buy you and your slimy partner dinner, then you are gonna have to get wet and get off your fat ass to give it to me!"

I guess this pissed him off, too, as you should have seen the look on his face when he approached my window that I had rolled down about six inches. He slapped the ticket on the outside of my wet window and said, "See you in court, kid."

I then carefully peeled the soaked ticket from the outside of my window hoping not to tear it or ruin the ink bearing the officer's name and badge number.

Now I was pissed off and I wanted my day in court. I phoned the court and explained that I needed my court date moved up because I was relocating to Las Vegas in mid-January.

They obliged and upon entering the court building at 26th and California I saw this guy seated on one of those old wrap around school chairs with a hand written sign above his head that read "Attorney." It also had an arrow pointing at him.

I explained that I had this ticket and he looked at the calendar on the wall and said, "I can beat this ticket for $50."

I said okay and I stood there thinking he would send me somewhere to explain my story to my new lawyer. He then said, "Well, you got da fifty?"

So I peeled off a fifty dollar bill from my wad and dropped it on his wrap-around desk top. I then explained I needed to be called first because I had taken half a day off work and didn't want to sit there all day. He said, "Yeah, yeah, just go to courtroom 14 and sit down."

When I walked into the courtroom, it was packed with the locker room stench courtesy of Cook County. I was able to squeeze in somewhere in the back of the room.

All of the sudden the clerk called my name first and I stood up looking all around for my lawyer but he was nowhere to be found. The clerk then motioned for me to sit back down, which I did.

For the next minute my mind went crazy. How can I be so stupid to give this guy $50? He probably wasn't even a lawyer and now he was gone with my 50 dollar bill and probably a few more. What a great scam, I thought, and felt like an idiot.

Then the back courtroom door opened and I heard hustling footsteps up the center aisle. Then I felt a slap on my back and heard, "Let's go kid."

It was him, my brilliant lawyer, except now he had on a tie and sports coat. What a relief! We walked up in front of the judge and the judge said, "Mr. Jones your client was caught doing 74 MPH in a 55...how do you plead?"

"Not guilty, your honor!"

The Judge then said, "On what grounds?"

My lawyer replied, "My client was merely doing 55 in a 55, your honor."

The Judge then struck the gavel and said, "Dismissed!"

My jaw dropped as I looked around for those crooked coppers. I thought I would be able to tell the judge about the way they shook me down. I thought maybe they would lose their jobs at the very least. I wanted my day in court, but today it would be no such luck.

My lawyer then said,"Go wait outside in the hall and I will get you your license back."

Moments later he handed me my driver's license and his business card and said, "Was that quick enough for you? I specialize in DUIs so if you ever get jammed up again just give me a call."

On the way home from the courthouse it all sunk in. No wonder all the Chicago Coppers want to work traffic. The way the system is there is no justice. My dad was right...it is all bullshit.

As it turns out, it is cheaper to pay them off in the street because the lawyers and judges are in on the take anyway. Let's see... $20 in the street to a couple crooked coppers or $50 to a crooked lawyer and scumbag judge, not to mention the half day of pay you lose. You do the math. Good old Chicago.

My parents had mixed emotions about me leaving Chicago, and so did I. I explained that this was the chance of a lifetime. They knew I had always wanted to be a Chicago cop, but it just wasn't meant to be. It was the height of affirmative action, and I wasn't the right color or gender at the time. Besides, Las Vegas was calling and I got the job all on my own. No payoffs or graft were involved, and it felt good. Deep down my parents were proud of me, but they really didn't want to see me go. I knew I could always come back home if things didn't work out. I loved my parents and my whole family, but this was truly the chance of a lifetime and I just had to go. I was so excited I couldn't sleep.

So around the 10th of January my dad helped me pack up my stereo and two polyester suits into my 1978 Chrysler Cordova and we headed west. I was so excited that we damn near drove straight through from the south side of Chicago to the Las Vegas Strip. I had the name of a Chicago copper named Billy who was a friend of another Chicago copper named Billy who I had grown up with. Billy said he would put me up for a few days. The guy was staying at some fleabag hotel near the Strip and he said I could "bed down" there until I found an apartment. It was a one-bedroom dump and two crazy bachelors already lived there. Now there were three: Billy, Larry, and me.

I slept on a beanbag chair on the floor, Larry slept on the couch, and Billy had the bed. My dad and I went to the Tropicana hotel for dinner on my birthday and he jumped on a flight that night back to Chicago. He was crying at the airport as he said goodbye. It was only the third time in my life that I had seen him cry. The other two times were when Kennedy died when I was 8 years old, and when he got a phone call that his older brother Eddie had died in a car wreck in Stevens Point, Wisconsin. At the airport I acted like Mr. Tough Guy but as soon as I lost sight of my dad down the walkway I cried like a baby. To this day I don't think I ever told him.

So there you have it. My mind in early 1980 was ready for a change. I needed to get away from Chicago, at least for a while. I needed to go out on my own and "sink or swim" in a new city with a new challenge.

Officer Rusin, Las Vegas METRO Police Department...it had a nice ring to it.

Note: Make no mistake here...I loved Chicago and especially my south side neighborhood. However, I had already swallowed my pride and the pill that professional hockey was not in my future. So I resorted to Plan B. I wanted to be a cop and put my degree to work. I thought I needed a fresh, clean start and Las Vegas was interested in me. No payoffs were involved; the job was offered not because of who I knew or who knew me. No, it was just me, and it felt good. I knew I could always come back home if things didn't work out. Sure, I would miss my friends and my family, but going to a new city like Las Vegas excited me and would officially begin my real law enforcement career. I would be one of the good guys wearing the white hat. Besides, ever since my college days I always had illusions of becoming a Fed with ATF. This would be a great stepping stone to make it to the "bigs". It all seemed so right!

LVMPD

Las Vegas. Two short words that mean so much. Money, sex, gambling, extortion, drugs, pimps, whores, loan sharks, suicide, bail bondsmen, scams, thieves, the mob, mystique, corruption, murder, booze, and the "action" never stops. Just think about it; no last call! It's going strong 24 hours a day, 365 days a year. What a town! What a place to be young and single! What a place to be in a police uniform! Take it from me; it's one of the coolest jobs on Earth. Simply put, there's no place like Las Vegas.

That's precisely why, as a 25-year-old "young" single guy from Chicago, I wanted to be a part of it. But I wanted to be on the good side. That is why, in January, 1980, I became one of Las Vegas's Finest. We were known as METRO, and I am proud to say that this one small word, METRO, struck fear into the hearts of many a crook, and it still does to this very day. There is truly no finer police department in all the land.

Proudest Moment

The day after I arrived, on January 16, 1980, I was sworn in as a METRO police officer and it was one of the proudest days of my life. Any cop will tell you that. In retrospect, I wish my Dad would have stayed to watch it, but I really didn't know beforehand that it would be so cool. I raised my right hand and swore before God and country that I would uphold the law and the constitution, and then I was presented with my badge and ID. I will never forget how that beautiful gold badge shined. It had the number 2063 inscribed on its back, which was my badge number and what I, Officer Rusin, would be called for the next four years.

A rookie cop immediately becomes part of the greatest fraternity on Earth. Of course, every rookie is tested repeatedly in their first year by veterans, but we all look forward to the test; first as a "ride along" partner then to the Police Academy. Every new officer is constantly reminded during their first year that they are "just a rookie".

Young, Dumb, and Full of...

I was sworn in as Las Vegas Police Officer on January 16, 1980. That day we went to the police range to learn how to shoot and qualify with our service weapons, 9 millimeter Smith & Wesson semi-automatic hand guns.

When I got to Las Vegas, I didn't even know what street I was on and I had never even fired a gun before. My first night on duty I had to ask one of the older cops how to put my gun belt on. His name was Wayne and he helped me a lot; he told me to buy a map!

One day, I was in uniform as a "ride along" prior to the academy when I got a phone call from some attorney named Dominic from Chicago. I answered the phone and this Dominic guy says, "Mr. Rusin, I understand that you paid off Don for the Chicago Fireman's job and we would like you to come back to Chicago and testify about this payoff." Dead silence on my end. I think I was in shock!

I told him that I was a police officer in Las Vegas now and I didn't know what he was talking about. Dominic went on to say that they were after the corrupt politicians and I would not be charged. He insisted that they would grant me immunity, because all they wanted was Don.

I thought to myself that I didn't really want to take a bullet in the back of my head at such a young age among the skyscrapers near the Federal building in sweet home Chicago. The Chicago River scene with the cement boots also came back to mind.

Sweat started to pour down my face as I again said, "I'm sorry but I don't know what you're talking about."

About three months later Dominic called again and left a message for me to call him back, so I did. This time, Dominic had more specific information, but I again told him that I still didn't know what he was talking about. I asked him not to call back unless he had a subpoena or warrant. Thank God he never did. He obviously was on a "fishing expedition" trying to get someone to flip. I understand nobody ever did and that asshole Don remained in office for the next 25 years.

As rookies, we were "lowly ride-alongs" until the academy began in late February. We were teamed up with senior officers and handled calls mostly as observers, unless, of course, something really bad was going down. I was teamed up in the beginning with some guy named Steve who turned out to be a real "Jagoff".

Steve was a phony bastard from some Podunk town who thought he was hot shit. To me he was just a hillbilly with a gun and a badge, but I had to play the game.

Let's just say if it was a construction job back in Chicago he would have "accidentally" caught a shovel in the back of his head.

One night after our shift, the Sergeant wanted to see me alone in his office. I really liked our Sergeant and he turned out to be a great guy. Hell, he ended up being Sheriff. That is how great Jerry was. He was seated at his desk and I was standing on the other side of it when he began his dissertation. "You know Rusin, if you don't want this job, just put your gun and badge on my desk and get the fuck outta here!"

I was stunned. I said, "Sarge, what are you talking about?"

"Officer Steve said you went to a bar call tonight and you sat on a bar stool!"

A million thoughts went through my head and so I blurted the best, most well thought out articulate words my south side Chicago mind could come up with:

"That's bullshit Sarge!"

I then laid into the Sarge as best I could, "My ass may have touched or leaned up against the bar stool, but give me a break, Sarge, I moved here from Chicago for this job. I went to school for this job. I haven't even been to the academy yet. I don't even know what street I am on half the time or how to even stand in my uniform...and you are busting my balls because that asshole Steve said I was sitting on a bar stool? What kind of Mickey Mouse department is this?" I said incredulously. "No, I am not giving up my badge and gun unless you make me, Sarge. It's just not fair.... and another thing...I ain't ridin' with that Jagoff piece of shit Steve anymore!"

The Sarge just smiled as if he liked what I had to say. I guess I passed his silly little test of standing up for myself. The Sarge was cool. "OK Rusin, I'll give you another chance."

"Thanks Sarge" I said.

And as I walked to my locker I thought to myself...no wonder cops drink! Not only do you have to worry about the bad guys, even some of your so-called partners will throw you under the bus. Needless to say I avoided hillbilly Steve from that day on!

About a week later, I was teamed up with a pretty cool training officer named Ron and we were getting along pretty good when the Sarge came over the radio saying that he would be out at a disturbance at the Pizza Hut on Maryland Parkway. It just happened to be our patrol beat that night.

Ron, who was driving our car, started to head that way when all of the sudden the same Sarge came back on the radio asking for help quickly; it was obvious from his voice that this was serious. He sounded like he might be in some trouble as he was huffing and puffing, struggling to get his words out. Ron squealed to a stop as he turned into the Pizza Hut lot. There I observed four biker-types fighting with the Sarge.

Here we go, I thought to myself.

My hockey instincts just took over and I immediately dove across the hood of our squad car and grabbed one biker, pulled him down to the pavement with his vest over his head, and cuffed him, face down. I got up and started beating the shit out of the biker who was engaged with the Sarge, as Ron had another guy he was wailing away at. When the dust settled, all four bikers were tuned up pretty good and they were soon off to jail care of the METRO meat wagon. The adrenaline rush was fun and made me feel like a kid again. Truth be told, it really felt great being on the METRO team!

I had a cut lip and scraped knee, and my shirt and trousers were ripped up a bit, but it was my moment to shine Chicago-style. The Sarge thanked me profusely and we laughed as he said, "Rusin, you might not know how to stand at a bar call yet, but you sure know how to fight."

When he said that, I smiled so bright that my newly cut lip hurt. Ron and the Sarge just laughed.

That night at debriefing, the Sarge made a public statement in front of my entire squad that made me feel like a million bucks. He said, "Don't you guys mess with Rusin!" I wasn't sure if that meant I was some kind of "badass" or that I was now on "his team." Either way, it felt good!

It got me instant respect among my peers, and the timing couldn't have been more perfect. Things were definitely looking up.

The Academy

The Academy is like 12 long weeks of "Hell Night." They put so much pressure on you just to try to get you to crack. They really want you to quit, because that means you didn't want to be a cop bad enough to begin with. They put you through physical, mental, and emotional torment; you name it, they do it. They figure that if you can't take it in a controlled setting, what will you do when you are on the street in the real world? My academy staff was cold blooded and they were masters at getting in our faces and making stuff up. When one of the recruits was about to be let go from the program, they would hang a cutout of a black hand in front of the mirrored window for all of us students to see. Then they would place a mouse in their boa constrictor's cage, and when the snake swallowed the mouse, they would turn the hand around and the other side would be white. The back door of the academy classroom would open, and one of the staff would slowly walk up and down each aisle until he came to the unlucky recruit who was about to be fired. He would stop behind the soon-to-be-jobless one and place his right hand wearing a white glove on the right shoulder of the "poor wannabe street soldier", and then escort him or her out the back door. That was it; we would never see that recruit ever again. It was cold blooded, but very effective!

Most of the time, we knew it was coming since the test scores were posted and no recruit was allowed to fall below 80%, ever. Also, the "gigs" were posted, and if you received more than 36, you were let go. Gigs were handed out for "allegedly" improper behavior or not passing inspection perfectly or not saying, "Sir, yes sir!" at every response. It was a way to mess with the recruits and add pressure to try to get us to crack.

If you did well on all the tests, they would make your life miserable by laying a bunch of gigs on you. One time, I remember the Sergeant got in my face and said I had some egg on my face. I said, "But sir, I don't eat eggs, sir."

That improper remark, although true, cost me 25 pushups and three gigs. I earned 33 gigs in the first nine weeks of training, so I had to sweat it out for the last three weeks. I would always get a gig for my boots not being shiny enough. I never shined my boots harder during those first nine weeks. Then I got smart. I found Jesse, the shoeshine guy at the Riviera Hotel, and he would shine my boots every night and place them in plastic bags. It cost me $5 a day but I got in line. I graduated with exactly 36 gigs, but I never let them see me sweat. That's the Chicago way!

I vividly recall one funny morning while standing in line outside for inspection at 7a. The Sarge gets in my face - 2 inches from my nose and screams, "Officer Rusin, who shined your boots?" I responded honestly, "Sir, Jesse shined my boots, Sir!" "JESSE?" he screamed back, as particles of his spit hit my face!

"And who in the hell is Jesse?" "Sir, Jesse is the shoe shine guy and shithouse attendant at the Riviera Hotel, Sir!" With that honest response I had him! He busted out laughing right in my face as did I and all my other classmates. It was beautiful as the Sarge made a quick exit back into the building trying not to let us see him laugh. He told me about a year later he laughed his ass off once he got inside the building. It was a classic!

Graduation day was the best feeling in the world! Only 24 of the initial 40 recruits graduated, so they had weeded out 16 of the original crop. Those of us who made it to the end were ready to hit the streets with a training officer and learn to become a real cop. At least, we thought we were ready. And it felt great.

I wrote this poem around the time of our academy graduation:

Las Vegas METRO Police Academy – 1980

Pitchford, Sugden, Scholl and Conner...
These are the men we were forced to honor

This experience I'm sure we will never forget...
And together as a class we should never regret

It all started in February on the 26th day...
As we all looked forward to the 16th of May

Some of us breezed, for a few it was fun...
But to most it seemed like mid-May would never come

But we ran and crawled and today we still stand...
We should all walk tall 'cause we've conquered our demand

There were ups and downs, but think of the good days
we had...
When the test scores came out some were happy, some sad

But our common bond is that we all have our pride...
Be happy with the goods and take the bads in stride

We tip our hats to this fine Academy Staff...
For the first six weeks we never saw one laugh

We thank these great men for the memories and the fun...
The gauntlet, push-ups, crab crawl and the 5-mile run

The inspections were a drag that most of us hated...
For our appearance and memory we had to be rated

"Take a gig on your weapon and what's this string?"
"Gimme twenty-five, you're disgusting!"
But you don't say a thing

"Your shoes don't shine and there's egg on you face!"
"Your hair's a mess, you're a total disgrace!"

So you bite your lip and you say, "Sir, Yes Sir!"
You don't even eat eggs and shiny your shoes were

And as the gigs add up, you try not to crack....
When will this Staff get off your back?

As the weeks go by you count every day
You'll be so happy on the 16th of May

So be proud, walk tall, it wasn't easy you know...
We've conquered our mission, for we are METRO!

Badge #2063

I remember the night of our graduation well. We had the reception at the Las Vegas cop-owned bar called the Debriefing Room. We all partied and drank our asses off. A couple of my graduating buddies and I went outside for some fresh air and we stopped to mess with a guy at the bottom of the stairs. A couple of us told the seemingly-drunken bastard to "hit the road." I remember that one of us shoved him in the direction of the sidewalk and said, "Keep walking!" We thought we were hot shit. It turns out that the drunkard was one of the Deputy Chiefs coming up the stairs to be the keynote speaker for the graduation ceremony. You should have seen the looks on our faces when he was introduced! We all went to the back of the room and hoped that he was too drunk to remember who we were and that we had ever messed with him. Luckily for us, it turned out that he was too drunk.

After the reception, a couple of us went to the MGM Grand to gamble with one of our first METRO paychecks. My buddy "Buffalo Mark" and I lost everything we had. I remember driving home early the next morning rather drunk with not one thin dime in my pocket thinking to myself that this was a tough town.

Lieutenant Cocksucker

I had just gotten my brand new business cards and boy, was I hot shit. Fresh out of the Academy, I had just completed my field training program. I was fitting in pretty good with the swing shift I was assigned to and was making some great new friends.

One night I stopped in to one of our favorite watering holes called Good Time Charlie's which was on Maryland Parkway just next to Sunrise Hospital. Happy hour mixed drinks were just fifty cents and all the hot nurses from Sunrise went there when they finished their shift. Nurses were always clean and a lot of fun to hang around with. I guess it's because they all had honorable jobs and had to deal with a lot of crap and carnage like us coppers.

Sitting at the bar, sipping my drink of choice, which was Christian Brothers Brandy and Ginger Ale, Johnny the bartender introduced me to some guy named Richie who claimed to be a bodyguard for Lola Falana, who was a pretty big deal in Vegas in the early 80s. We shot the shit for an hour or so and I gave him a new business card of mine and that was that.

About a week later, after my 10-hour shift was over my Sergeant said, "The Lieutenant wants to talk to you after debriefing." I thought that was a little strange.

I had never spoken to the Lieutenant before, so I thought it might be a "welcome" ritual for new cops to meet and greet the boss the next level up in our chain of command; my boss's immediate boss. I never smelled a rat until I saw the look on the Lieutenant's face when he said, "Come on in and close the door."

As I entered his office, up close he looked like the fat, red-headed weirdo I had heard he was. Some of the guys had warned me to be careful around him; "He is a real cocksucker" they said.

No sooner did my ass hit the chair, when the Lieutenant began reading me my Miranda rights. I just sat there thinking this was some crazy rookie joke; maybe an extension of those silly academy pranks I had just lived through.

"Do you understand your rights?" He asked.

I said flippantly, "Yeah, yeah, sure Lieutenant... whatever," as I was looking for the candid camera.

"Rusin, do you think this is some kinda joke?" he asked.

I responded carefully "No, Lou...is it?"

The Lieutenant then led in, "Do you know a guy named Curly Pipher?"

"No sir, that name doesn't ring a bell," I said.

"You don't know Curly Pipher?" he asked again.

"No," I said, "I don't know anyone by that name." The Lieutenant just glared at me.

"What's this all about, anyway...Lou?" I asked.

He then put a photo in front of me of the same guy I had met at Good Time Charlie's the week before, who I only knew as "Richie".

"Oh dis guy, yeah I met him once at Good Time Charlie's about a week ago, but he said his name was Richie."

Again the Lieutenant just glared at me. "You know the vice squad did a warrant last night at his house and got twelve keys and a stash of guns."

"No, I don't know, but that's great Lou! A nice pinch," I opined.

He then placed my business card next to the photo and said, "He claims he got the guns from you."

I said, "That's bullshit!"

"Then how'd he get this?" pointing at my business card. I was speechless, knowing all along this was some kind of a "set up" or just a common way of someone in trouble to try and deflect the heat.

"I gave it to him when I met him," I answered.

"You know if this is true you are looking at some serious time off here," the Lieutenant stated.

"Time off?" I responded. "Lou, if this is true you can take my badge and gun and lock me up because I don't deserve to be a police officer."

In retrospect, this was a rather bold statement of only one who would tend to be innocent. "Will you take a polygraph test?" the fat beady-eyed bastard asked.

"Of course I'll take a polygraph, and do me a favor and hurry up because I want this bullshit behind me," I insisted.

"OK, I will set it up for tomorrow at 3 p.m."

Little did I know that word had spread like wildfire throughout the department that I could be in some kind of trouble. I walked out of the Lieutenant's office looking like a ghost and met up with some of the guys on my squad who had hung around to wait for me. I said, "This prick Lieutenant has me taking a polygraph test tomorrow."

Nick from New York, who was our police union guy, was livid. He told me. "No fuckin' way! You ain't takin' no polygraph test until the fuckin' punk with the cocaine and guns passes one first. Fuck the Lieutenant, that cocksucker!" I loved Nick and hated to let him down.

I felt so dumb and naïve at the time, but Nick was right. In reality, in my rookie state, I was intimidated by my chain of command and coerced to take this test. Even though I knew I didn't give this guy the guns, what if the polygraph came back "bad" or "inconclusive", even worse what if they had their own guy (the polygraph operator) say it came out "bad" just to send me packing back to Chicago?

But I had already told the Lieutenant that I would take the test. How would it look if I backed out now? The one question still remained that I had to sleep on that night. What kind of police department would have one of their own sworn law enforcement officers, take a polygraph exam before the slime ball drug-dealing, gun-toting arrestee does?

In any event, I took and passed the polygraph test the next day with flying colors, but it was hard for me to look at my Lieutenant ever again. And Dan if you are reading this, shame on you and the boys were right..."You are a cocksucker!"

Sniper

Fresh out of the academy I was driving our squad car westbound on Tropicana approaching Paradise Road, trying to prove to my training officer Larry that I could soon drive solo. Larry was a real laid back cat from West Virginia. I affectionately called him "Jethro" and he called me "Chicago Slick" or just "Slick" for short. He was a great guy and we often found humor wherever we could. We were both big Elvis fans so we would sing Elvis songs together to pass the time while on patrol and try to stump each other with a next verse of some of the "oldies." It kept us always in a good mood.

All of the sudden the shrill beep alerted all cars and the dispatcher announced, "All units, there is a report of a sniper in the tower at McCarren Airport."

I immediately got in the left lane, cracked a U-turn over the median strip and stepped on the gas, now traveling eastbound on Tropicana. Larry says, "Hey Einstein, McCarren is the other way."

I said, "I know! If you think I am driving up to a sniper in a big ass tower in a marked unit you are crazier than a shithouse rat! Hell, why don't we just stop at Earl Schieb's first and get a quick bullseye painted on the top of our squad car?"

No sooner did I finish my brief dissertation when our sane

Sarge came over the radio and stated, "All marked units stay away from McCarren at least two miles...we are sending in unmarked units."

I just smiled, then I belted out, "Who is the fuckin' training officer in this car anyways? Well at least someone around here has a brain besides me, huh Jethro?"

Jethro just thought for a few seconds and said, "That is why you will probably be the Sheriff some day!"

I was on a roll. "Nice try...and don't think I missed your sarcastic tone referring to me as Einstein!" Larry said, "Oh, you caught that?" I then baited Larry and said, "The boys are gonna love this one at debriefing. Then again, if you were to spring for lunch tonight I could come down with a minor case of amnesia."

"Forever?" Larry asked.

I smiled back..."That will cost you two lunches."

"Damn Rusin, you really are from Chicago."

"Yessir, I am."

Pretty Prostitutes

Most people think that prostitution is legal in Las Vegas. It is not. However, in reality it is big business in Las Vegas and part of the intrigue, excitement, and mystique of Sin City. The fact is that prostitution is illegal in the entire County of Clark, in which Las Vegas is located.

It's actually kind of crazy because in other Nevada counties like Nye, one can drive to Pahrump and find Sheri's Ranch, where it is legal.

In Sin City, laws are rather toothless if ever enforced, and the pimps and their whores (hoes) know it. In my opinion, it is because most residents don't frequent the strip that the ordinance is rarely enforced, as it tends to draw more tourists to play and stay.

However, METRO does crack down from time to time; especially on the "trick roll" experts because they give the town a bad name. These honeys usually lurk in casinos and try and find the "high rollers" to hit on. Fake seductive eye contact can lure the men over to the casino bar where drinks are downed, usually by the men only, as the girl wants to stay sober to pull off her heist. Stupid, drunk men who don't watch their drinks like hawks are the easiest of prey. The next thing they know, their room becomes a crime scene as the man might be pleasured in an altered state. If and when he passes out the honey is gone with the money, casino chips, Rolex, or whatever else she can steal. Of course, she is long gone by the time the now-poorer idiot ever comes to. Rarely do these victims call METRO as they are embarrassed, usually married, and they just opt to make a room burglary report for say a Rolex or wedding ring for insurance purposes and other obvious reasons.

Hotels will show the victim their "black book" of thieves, and if they can identify the suspect METRO will be notified and file a report. The next time she is stopped she will be questioned harshly and jailed every time for "loitering for the purpose of prostitution," a misdemeanor.

The street walkers are your lowest class hoes and almost all have pimps. They are out all night grabbing $50 -$100 a pop for oral sex. Most are dirty and nasty druggies from broken homes. They can't come home each night with less than $500. Otherwise, they catch a beating. It is a horrible existence and quite sad.

Some of these cleaner girls will part with a $50 bill to pay off security wherever they can to be allowed to sit inside. It is a step up from the street scene and most of these customers have a hotel room to go to.

The next level would be your inside girls, who are a bigger step up in class and know how the game is played. I would say that it is 50/50 that they have a pimp. A lot of these sweethearts only come to Vegas on weekends to make their thousands and then go back home. They rely on valets, pit bosses, bartenders, and club doormen to give them a call when they have "action". This way the call comes in for a date, the date is screened as not a METRO cop, and the scene is set usually knowing the time, hotel, and room number. This becomes very lucrative for the set up guy because these call girls go from $250/hour to $2,000-$3,000 a night. The kickbacks are amazing and usually 10%. These guys clean up during super bowl, prize fights, and other big events.

Some of the classy strippers in town can also be had, but they ain't cheap and mostly high rollers and "whales" pick them up through going to the strip clubs or their VIP host at the hotel where they are staying; usually in the penthouse suite!

Note: A "whale" is one of the highest rated gamblers with at least a million dollar credit line and up. Everyone wants to be a whale!

Enforcement efforts regarding our "hoe patrol" were a really fun and always interesting detail. The Sarge would team two of us up usually every night to handle the assignment. We would park a large METRO police bus behind the old Frontier Hotel that seated roughly 50-60 passengers — maximum. We would then rove the strip grabbing hoes off the street for breaking the Nevada Revised Statute for "loitering for the purpose of prostitution". It was a bullshit misdemeanor charge but it pissed the girls off as we would tie them up with "processing" before we transported them to jail. As each strip-assigned patrol car would pick up a hoe or two, they would simply drop them off at the big bus. This kept the patrol units on patrol. The busload was timed to roll downtown at half shift or for the next five hours or so, as we worked 10 hour shifts. Basically, we got them off the street and that "down time" cost them money, and more importantly, pissed off their pimps. That was the best part.

It was easy to spot the hoes a mile away. There were usually alone, dressed up with "CFM" high heels and a tiny purse usually hanging off their shoulder. You could also walk through any casino and pick them out at the bars lurking for some action. If it was in any way questionable we did not take a chance and approach. Our motto was that when it came to hoes and a misdemeanor charge whenever questionable…"tomorrow's another day!"

Basically, it was all a game and nobody ever complained.

My partners and I would not tolerate fist fighting on the bus because one of the poor hoes just sitting there might have gotten injured with a wild punch. Hence, we would move the combatants to the parking lot and let them go toe to toe. Needless to say, we had a front row seat for some knockdown drag out fights that would rival Hearns vs. Hagler as the bus load of hoes would be going wild! It didn't happen a lot, but when the Sarge caught wind of it he just shook his head and said, "No more." And that was that.

If the volume of hoes got heavy, we would make three or four trips downtown at quicker intervals to accommodate the booking process. I was offered oral sex every night on many occasions, but never bit. The hoes figured if they spent 10-15 minutes in the desert blowing a cop to let them go, they were ahead of the game. They were not stupid when it came to us wasting their time for five hours. They figured they could give a cop a "freebie" and get back to work. You do the math. In all honesty, I never heard of a METRO officer partaking in a "quid pro quo" as such. Not to say that it never happened.

The most amazing thing about the hoes (and I got to know a lot of them) is that they would never give up their pimps. Some would lie and say they didn't have one. A few probably weren't lying. I always tried to treat them respectfully, but sometimes it was hard. I played the long game hoping they would talk to me when some nasty shit went down on the strip, like an armed robbery or murder, and they would confide in me to furnish a lead. It actually worked a few times, as the hoes knew the streets better than anyone.

The last thing I would like to say is that the hoes did not mess with METRO. They respected us for the most part, or at least pretended to, and that was fine by me.

Street Whores and Snitches

One of the things I could never understand was how these Las Vegas pimps got a hold of these street whores. I mean, the whores would run all day and night long selling sex and then give all their earnings to some black pimp, who would in turn treat her like shit. It was fascinating talking to these women. Most of the white whores talked like they were black. I guess you do emulate your boss, after all.

Most of the whores who walked the Strip were out trying to earn an honest living, and believe it or not, most cops respected the honest ones to a certain extent. It was the thieves and trick roll artists that we were after.

Some of my funniest and weirdest calls were from the four years when I worked the Strip.

One time, I was called to the Desert Inn Hotel for an attempted murder situation. They had a white male in custody who allegedly attempted to cut some black whore's throat with a broken and jagged champagne bottle. I looked at the blond haired young man in his clean tennis outfit, and when I looked at the black-wigged whore who just smiled at me. She said, "Hey officer Rusin, how's it going?" I just shook my head and laughed. I had arrested this black transvestite before on a prostitution charge. I went back to the "pretty boy" suspect and asked him what had happened. This was his story:

"I was sitting at the blackjack table when I spotted this good looking girl at the bar. We made eye contact and she signaled me over. She said she would perform oral sex on me for $50, so I took her up to my room. We drank some champagne and she started to blow me. When I looked down, I saw him "jacking himself off." Surprise, surprise I thought to myself. Mind you, I tried to keep a straight face when I heard this.

"I got furious so I freaked out and grabbed the champagne bottle and broke it over the chair. I tried to cut him but he ran out of the room screaming for security. I chased him down the hall and out to the pool area when security grabbed me and arrested me."

I then asked him what he thought should happen now? He said, "I just want my money back!"

I knew the black transvestite didn't want any part of this so I acted as his new lawyer and judge and gave him the following advice:

"Let me get this straight. You agreed to pay $50 for a blow job and you got your blow job, correct?"

He said, "Well, yeah."

"There was no fine print that this "thing" you picked up had to be a girl, was there?" I asked.

He sheepishly said, "No."

I said I was going to take the handcuffs off of him, and if I were him, I would just forget the whole matter or he would be the one going to jail for attempted murder. He agreed to forget the $50 and get lost.

The black transvestite thanked me for not getting him tied up for the night with swearing out a complaint, which would have cost him a night of work and a headache. Besides, he wanted to go and look for his next trick so he could make a little more money. And as he left the property I asked him to do me a favor..."please refrain from jerking off when blowing your clients!" He said with a smile, "OK, Rusin."

That hotel was a regular stop for us, and another crazy call from that same hotel went like this:

A guy thought he wanted to make a police report, so I got called to the scene. This big fat white guy smoking a big fat cigar was thumbing through the hotel "whore book" when I arrived. He said that some young honey had rolled him for $30,000 cash. I thought, "What a bunch of bullshit."

Then he said he picked up this chick at the bar and took her out to his car in the parking lot for a $50 blow job. He said that while his pants were down around his ankles she must have rifled through his left front pocket and grabbed his $30,000 cash.

I said, "Sir, I can't believe you can fit that kind of cash in your front pants pocket."

He said as matter of fact, "Oh yeah you can if you carry all thousands."

Up until that night I had never even seen a thousand-dollar bill before. He then said, "It's a good thing she didn't get this pocket," as he pulled a two inch wad of thousand dollar bills from his other front pocket. He then pulled another two inch wad out of his back pocket. I just sat there in amazement as I looked at the thousand dollar bills. Eighty one thousand dollar bills were in front of me on the security office desk. I said, "Sir, are you crazy? Why don't you lock this money up in the cage and just pull markers?"

He said he wasn't crazy, and told me he owned all the land down Sahara Blvd. east of the Strip. He was a sports book gambler and he needed the money on hand. This crazy bastard was running around with $110,000 cash in his pockets. I could just imagine how happy that thieving hooker was when she looked at the wad of bills she had stolen! Talk about Merry Christmas in July!

He didn't want to sign a complaint, and he never did pick his sweetheart out of the whore book, so he said to forget about it. He just didn't want the next guy who couldn't afford it to get taken like that. I thanked him for his concerns and said, "Adios." Of course on both of these Desert Inn calls I hit security up for a complimentary round of golf and a one hour massage. That was standard procedure when you took care of the hotels without getting any bad publicity. The old "you scratch my back and I'll scratch yours" mentality. Besides, most of the security guards and bosses were former coppers from somewhere, and they all knew the drill.

The one hotel I had the most problems with was Caesar's Palace. That security force was the biggest bunch of thieves around. They would put "the arm" on all the working girls for $50 a night, just to sit there and be allowed to work. The girls that didn't pay would get tossed, and then they would call us to press charges and take the girls downtown for a bullshit "loitering for the purpose of prostitution" charge. Security always liked us to come around the back and go directly to the security room where the girl who refused to pay them off was seated. Not me. I would park in front by the main entrance next to the fancy fountains and walk through the three casino bars collecting all the whores I could find. These whores would be pissed off because they had already paid off security the $50 for the night to be left alone. Sometimes I would have 20 girls with me and I would take them all downtown. I didn't like being used as the muscle for the security force when the girls wouldn't pay them off. It stunk, but when I got a couple of girls to agree to wear a wire and work as informants, I was force transferred off the Strip for a while. I didn't realize that the Chief of Security at that time was our Sheriff's golfing buddy. Oh well, I was looking for a Federal job by then, anyway.

One other funny call at Caesar's was from an old man who claimed he got trick rolled for $1,000, all in $50 bills. He told me he was from California and that his son was a California Highway Patrol officer and his wife was playing blackjack in the casino. There was a young black whore in custody, and he claimed she stole his money when he took her up to his room for some oral sex. After the sex, he went into the bathroom and like a dummy left his pants with his wad of $50 bills near the whore. He claims he saw her run from the room and he put on his pants and chased after her. The elevator was slow so she was still in the hall. He grabbed her and called security. The old man was somewhat embarrassed but rather ballsy, I thought, to take some street whore up to his hotel room with his poor old wife gambling in the casino. Anyway, all he wanted was his money back.

I told him that if he wasn't willing to sign a complaint all I could do was bluff her and he understood. I went into the security room and the whore said she didn't take his money, but I knew she was lying. I said if she gave him back the money he wouldn't press charges. She stuck to her story and my bluff didn't work.

I went back to the old man and he said he didn't want to press charges because he didn't want his wife to know. I certainly understood that. Then he asked me to give it another try, and besides, I knew she was lying. This time I went into the room and told her to stand up and put her hands behind her back. Bad news for her, but the old man agreed to sign a complaint and now we were going downtown. It was my 2nd bluff. She knew now that she would be strip-searched, "cavities and all", and we would find the money. She also knew that if we found the money she would be tagged as a "thieving whore"— and believe me, in Vegas, no whores want that tag. METRO goes hard after the thieves because they give the town a black eye. Good, honest whores, on the other hand, add to the fun of visiting the famous Las Vegas. That's just a fact of life there.

I was getting ready to put the other bracelet on her when she said, "Wait, wait."

I knew I had her then. She asked if the money was found, would he still agree to drop the charges? I said, "I don't know, I would have to check with him."

I left the room and went back in and said, "If he gets all his money back, namely 20 tightly rolled $50 bills, he would agree to drop the charges."

She said, "Okay, then."

I took the handcuffs off of her and she put her foot on the chair and started to pull $50 bills out of her vagina. They were all wet and crinkled and she dropped them one by one on the desk in front of me until all 20 were there in a lovely pile.

I then did a field interview with her and listed her as a "thieving whore" so the boys would be on her from now on, anyway. If she could lie to METRO, we could lie to her. After all, she had just gotten the pass of her young life.

She thanked me and I let security escort her from the property. The old man was so thankful. The smile on his face said it all as he picked up all 20 of his wet, gooey, crinkled $50 bills. Again, justice served.

I remember one time we got called to the Las Vegas Hilton where a whore was wanting to turn her pimp in. This was virtually unheard of, because when the pimp got out of jail the whore would be dead. This young white girl was sick and tired of the beatings, and she showed us her back that had welts from being struck with a metal coat hanger and the cigarette burns on the back of her arms. She said her black pimp, Tyrone, would beat her and burn her every time she would come home with less than $500 in a night. My partner Don and I had her call Tyrone from the security phone while we listened in. I recall Tyrone reading her the riot act, telling her not to come home unless she had $500. We then took a ride to Ty's hotel room where they were staying. We went in and started to question Ty about what he said to his girl on the phone. In essence, Ty started to deny demanding her nightly take and physically hurting her.

Don and I worked Tyrone over a little and we called for every METRO cop working the Strip to stop by and take a look and take a shot at Tyrone. We just wanted to get his attention and scare him; to let him know that if anything happened to his girl, we would be coming to get him. He got the message. We then drove him to McCarren airport and put him on a plane for Phoenix. We told him that if we ever saw him again in our town he was going to get another beating. We never saw Tyrone again, and his whore was still alive the last time I heard.

I used to hate to have to chase a whore on foot. It was a pain in the ass and so disrespectful to the uniform. Usually they wouldn't run, because they knew we would catch them and they would catch a beating. I chased this one running whore about two blocks in front of the Barbary Coast, and when I finally caught her I put her in my squad car and we took a little ride.

We drove about three miles past the end of Las Vegas Blvd. way out in the desert somewhere. I didn't say a word and neither did she all the way there. I stopped in the desert and said, "Get out."

I also got out and grabbed her by the throat and slapped her across the face. Not hard but just to get her attention. I then draped her over the top of my car and said in my mean guy voice, "If you ever run from METRO again we will beat the shit out of you and bury you out here, do you understand?"

She said she did and I put her back into my patrol car and headed back to the bright lights of the Strip. On the way back, I bought her a soda at the 7-11 and a pack of smokes and let her out in front of the Barbary Coast where I had just caught her earlier. She said, "Ain't you takin me downtown?"

I said, "Nah, you've had enough for tonight." She just smiled and said "thank you Officer Rusin," and got out walking.

I'll be damned if the very next night I was parked on the Strip in traffic next to the curb with my windows rolled down and the same whore walked to my patrol car and let herself in. In fact, she had startled me because I never even saw her approaching the car. I acted like it was a test as I complimented her dress and said, "Now that's more like it."

I drove her to the Riviera Hotel and gave her a pass. This whore turned into one of my best snitches on the Strip. If anything ever went down on the Strip she would know about it and let me know. I don't even remember her name, but she was a good whore and thanks to her I made a few good felony arrests.

We used to book about 150-200 street whores a night during a 10-hour shift. We had the large METRO police bus parked behind the Frontier Hotel and all the patrol cars, along with the "meat wagon", would round up the whores. The meat wagon was just a large van that we would try and squeeze as many whores in as possible. The van's seating capacity was 16, and sometimes we would squeeze 20-24 girls in at one time. Mike and I held the record for a while as we stuffed three small whores behind the back seat. I still don't know how they fit back there. We would then find the ripest, dirtiest, smelliest vagrant and put him in with the whores and laughed as they all screamed.

We would make two runs downtown each night with the big bus full of whores. This would tie them up for at least five hours or more. That was our mandate, to keep them off the street, and this really pissed off their pimps.

Babes, Babes, and More Babes

You would not believe all the beautiful women in Las Vegas. I don't care if they are all implants; they are all over the place. I used the biggest scams to get the ladies, and I was not alone. Each of our squad cars had a computer terminal that would get us all kinds of good intelligence information. I used to troll the casino parking lots at shift change hours and watch the cocktail waitresses, showgirls, and casino workers walk to and from their cars. The hotels always liked METRO around, and besides, we ran the town.

I would see a good-looking lady walk to or from her car and I would"run" her car plates to get her name and home address. Then I would put that info into my little black book. I would also check her work card to see where she was employed and what she did.

If you were patrolling along and spotted a good looking girl you could run her plate and find out where she lived and worked in a few seconds.

The ladies would think nothing of seeing a patrol car in their casino parking lot and it made them feel safe. If they only knew.

I was no Don Juan but I was in uniform, and for some reason the women loved that METRO uniform. I am told they still do. I guess there are all kinds of groupies out there, and who was I to question if they liked the uniform or me? It really didn't matter as long as we had a good time.

You could stop a girl walking to her car and say hello or smile and they would almost always stop and talk to you. They would ask inquisitively what was up and you would make up some bullshit like there was a guy seen lurking in the area or ask them if they saw someone or show them a mug shot; anything to "break the ice." Of course, all I was trying to find out was if they were single and liked to drink.

METRO was well respected in that town, and rightly so. It was the best police department in the country, and besides, we had some cool looking uniforms. I would get at least two or three new "leads" every night. It was a smorgasbord atmosphere among the single guys. Hell, even some of the married guys did pretty good. But don't worry fellas, no names will be mentioned.

I and my two single cop roommates threw the best parties in Las Vegas. Don, Franky, and me had the cat's ass job and we were all young and single. We almost had to put a revolving door in front of our house. In four years we probably scored more than Wayne Gretzky.

We would pass out invitation flyers to every good looking girl we could find. I figured if you asked 300 girls to show up, odds were that the shindig would be smelling pretty good around midnight. Las Vegas is a town where you learn to play the odds to survive. If you focused your invitations on showgirls, cocktail waitresses, topless dancers, keno runners, hotel reservationists, and bartenders you had it covered. It never failed and more guys got laid thanks to me, Don, and Frankie. Those guys still owe us.

The best blast was without a doubt was in 1983 at the new MGM Grand just after it had reopened after the 1980 fire. We had the double penthouse suite going and food catered from the old Tower of Pizza. All the booze was "on the arm" and we would get the DJ from one of the topless joints to donate his time. It was either that or he would get locked up every night for cocaine possession, so he played along.

The room had a Jacuzzi and some sexual activity was going on in the private suite. Everywhere you looked there were babes, babes, and more babes. Word soon spread that we threw the best parties, because we did. Besides, who was going to tell us to turn down the music? Hell, the squad who was on duty even stopped by in uniform to pay their respects and hope it was still going strong after they got off shift. It always was. Those were some times, and after I left Las Vegas in 1983, that was what I missed most: the guys on METRO, the women, and the fun.

I Like the Night Life, Baby

New Year's Eve, the Super Bowl, and the world championship prize fights were some of the wildest times in Las Vegas. They would draw all the money in from all over, and the whores and thieves would follow. It is still that way and probably always will be. The traffic was always unbearable and the calls were backed up and weird as hell. A couple shootings would always seem to mar the festivities.

One of the best details I had was working Muhammad Ali's last fight on American soil in 1980, when he lost to Larry Holmes in the parking lot at Caesar's Palace. Mike and I had the meat wagon detail, so we parked near the back parking lot and took turns each round watching the action ringside. Just before the fight some idiot tried to jump over a 20-foot security fence and fell and broke his leg. We had to take him to the hospital before booking him, but we didn't go until the fight was over. I mean, the kid was screaming in pain and drunk in the back of the wagon. It was too bad for him, as Mike and I decided to stay and watch the fight. After all, this was Ali!

I remember yelling to him, "shut the fuck up...this is Ali!"

I also got a sweet gig when I was seated in the 10th row for the Larry Holmes v. Gerry Cooney fight, again at Caesar's in the parking lot, in 1982. That was some event, and I was seated next to Lola Falana. I couldn't help but stare at her. She caught me a couple of times, but I didn't care. She was the most beautiful black woman I had ever seen. When the fight was stopped I had to run up to Larry Holme's corner of the ring and make sure nobody got up there. I was in uniform and it is still cool seeing myself on the HBO reruns at the end of the fight.

A No Brainer

I remember this one call at the Circus Circus RV Park of a shooting and possible dead body. I was stopped at the traffic light at Riviera and Las Vegas Blvd. and so I was the first to arrive the scene. There were some people screaming and waving me over as I pulled my squad car into the RV back lot. I saw a body lying in the doorway of an RV trailer home with the legs inside, his ass on the stairs, and his back on the pavement. There was a shotgun between his legs, and it looked like he fell backwards out of the trailer. The only problem was that the guy's head was completely blown off and all I could see was the back part of his brain and a small valve over his throat sucking for air. It was a terrible sight that I will never forget.

I had beaten the paramedics there and wanted to help save this poor guy, but I didn't quite know what to do. In my cop mind I wanted to treat the scene like a staged homicide, as I wasn't 100% sure that it was a suicide. I walked up and I heard him gasping for air and also saw an almost perfect spray pattern of eyes, teeth, blood, and brain matter above the door on the walls and ceiling of the motor home. It appeared this poor guy had knelt down and wedged a 12-gauge shotgun between the floorboard and his throat and pulled the trigger. I had never seen so much bright red blood before, and when the paramedics got there this guy's vital signs were normal. The paramedics said there was no way for this guy to make it, so we just covered him with a sheet and called for the coroner. The only part that bothered me was that the breathing kept on for about 5 more minutes and a crowd was gathering as the paramedics stood there smoking and joking, so I asked for a my Sergeant to stop by. Sergeant Lem strolled by and took one look under the sheet and he had to be excused. It was that ugly.

The Sarge told the paramedics to take him to the hospital, but the guy died on the way and they were pissed because they had to get their sheets all bloody when they could have just waited for the coroner to take him to the morgue. The poor guy left a suicide note that said he had cancer so bad that he couldn't take the pain another day. But what a way to go. I had to call the Fire Department out to wash the blood from the pavement.

And as I drove away all I could think about were his poor kids (that were named in his suicide note). Now they would have to come and claim his RV with remnants of their Dad's blood, brains, eye particles and teeth on the ceiling and clean it up. I wish he would have just taken all the pills he had and just went to sleep.

Generally speaking, the dead bodies didn't bother me when they were older. I had a tough time seeing dead kids, especially babies. That is truly when the job gets tough and it can get to you. We try to be all macho but I assure you that is just an act.

I also hated the car wrecks with the mangled bodies. Especially when there were kids involved.

Cop Nails Kid in Crosswalk

Speaking of car wrecks and kids, I was patrolling in front of the Flamingo and a hot call came out as "a robbery in progress-man with a gun" at the 7-11 way south on the Strip at Warm Springs Road. I hung a u-turn over the median and headed southbound with my red lights flashing. I blew the light at Flamingo and Las Vegas Blvd. and was picking up speed. When I passed the Dunes I could see ahead that there was a mob of tourists across the street from the Aladdin hotel. I took my foot off the accelerator as a guy and a gal stepped into the crosswalk. But they stopped and saw me coming with my red lights flashing so I stepped back on the accelerator. I assumed they would wait for me to pass. Then, all of the sudden, they decided to run across the street. I jammed on my brakes and the guy froze in front of me like a deer in the headlights. I hit this poor kid with my squad car head on in what seemed like slow motion. He flew over my hood and his face hit my windshield as he continued over the top of my car about 30 feet to the curb. I saw him hit the pavement like a rag doll in my rear view mirror. Needless to say, I was horrified and I thought for sure I had just killed this poor guy. I was also a little pissed off because he actually ran in front of me. I got out of my car and ran to his aid. He was still breathing but was very shaken up. I could also see that his left leg was broken.

The fact that he was not dead made me want to hug this guy. Then his girlfriend came over and started to talk to me in her Chicago accent. The mob approached and I felt like a complete idiot for hitting a pedestrian in the crosswalk. Generally speaking, this is not good for a police officer to do.

The good news was that the kid from Chicago was going to be alright and I was relieved from duty pending an Internal Affairs investigation and accident investigation. I went back to the station and changed clothes, but I had to go and see this kid. I felt completely responsible and so sorry, so I went to Sunrise Hospital to pay my respects. The kid and his girlfriend knew I felt like shit and they were great about it. Like I said, we were all from Chicago.

I made sure that METRO picked up all of their hospital bills and paid them a healthy sum for their pain and suffering that I had caused. It was just one of those crazy things, and to this day I thank God that he wasn't dead. I had nightmares for years about the kid's face just before impact and his head bouncing off my windshield.

Believe it or not, I was exonerated during the investigation because a couple of witnesses said the kids actually ran in front of my patrol car.

It also helped that I was hustling to a hot call at the time, so it was understandable to the board that my intentions were proper given the circumstances and it was a total accident. Had I not been going to "a man with a gun" call, you can bet that my ass would have been hanging out to dry and rightly so.

Lie Detector Dogs

One of the funnier times I had on the job was the night we caught the appliance store burglars red handed. There had been a rash of appliance store burglaries in the area and the point of entry was always the same, so we figured it was the same crew. They would peel the back door on the bottom to avoid setting off the alarms. On this particular night they screwed up and the silent alarm sounded. METRO was there within minutes to find the felony crime in progress.

When I arrived in the alley behind the store, I noticed the bottom of the back door had been peeled up and there was a van parked in the alley with the engine running. I got the driver out of the van at gunpoint, handcuffed and proned him in the alley and got on the radio asking for some quick help as I knew the burglars were caught inside. Squad cars started showing up and a canine unit was also dispatched to the scene. The METRO canine core was amazing. All were beautifully trained Rottweilers who had the strongest bite of any dog on the planet.

We saw the burglars inside with our flashlights and we had the store surrounded. The owner showed up and opened the back door, and the canine handler let his dog in. Within minutes we had all three of our perps handcuffed and in custody. The dog grabbed one of the boys by the back of the collar and shook him around like a rag doll. It was something for all to see.

The canine handler then had a brilliant idea, as the four burglars were all handcuffed and face down in the alley. He told the boys that his dog was also trained in the art of lie detection; a four-legged polygraph expert who could tell immediately when you were lying. The only rule was that you had to look at the dog because he must see your eyes. We turned the handcuffed kids' heads to face the dog. Now, the thieves were already shook up but they weren't talking, so the first question was posed in the polygraph exam language.

"Is this the first time you boys ever stole anything?"

One kid said, "Yes!" and the dog growled with saliva coming out of his mouth and ran to within 10 inches of the kid's face.

The handler said, "Uh oh, I'm afraid that was a lie."

The next question was asked of another thief. "Did you boys burglarize Joe's Appliance last week Wednesday?"

The second boy answered "No," and again the dog growled and ran like a maniac drooling to within six inches of the screaming kid's face. Obviously it was another lie.

As luck would have it, the kids finally came around after our creative police work and told us where all the stolen appliances were being stored from their previous five burglaries. We returned what they had stolen and charged them all accordingly. Their testimony was not allowed because their lawyers claimed we violated their civil rights, and the judge agreed. We had recovered all the stolen property and knocked off the burglaries, so we had done our job. Besides, they were good kids who hopefully learned a valuable lesson that night. Don't mess with METRO and especially their smart, vicious dogs!

"The MGM Is Burning!"

Note: an edited version of this story was published in the 25th anniversary edition of the Las Vegas Review Journal in November, 2005. It is also available on the Wikipedia version of this tragic event.

I was already in plain clothes when the rear door of the METRO South substation burst open and Sergeant Martin yelled, "Jesus Christ, the MGM is burning!"

Everyone in the station got up and rushed to the door, hoping the Sarge was playing a sick practical joke. He wasn't.

Dark gray smoke was everywhere on the Strip and Flamingo Road. It was just after 7:15 on the morning of November 21, 1980, and the MGM Grand happened to be on my patrol beat.

We knew it was bad because we could hear sirens from all over town. My squad had just finished our 10-hour shift. We wanted to suit back up and hustle to the MGM, but the Sarge sent us home to get some sleep. As we walked to our cars, staring in disbelief at the smoke, the Sarge called out, "You guys stay close to your phones!"

All the while our relief squad — and every other vehicle equipped with lights and sirens within a 20-mile radius — was screaming toward the MGM.

As I pulled out of the station, I listened to the radio and watched the smoke billow above the Strip. By the time I got to my house in Green Valley, the death toll had reached 27 and counting, in just the first couple of hours. By the time I turned my TV on, reporters were live at the MGM, and there was no way I could sleep. My phone rang at about 11:00 a.m. and the desk sergeant told me to be back at the station by 3:00 p.m. to work a double. Little did I know then what the night would bring.

I got to the station about a half hour early. Word was spreading that we might run out of body bags. The fatality count had now topped 50, and a temporary morgue had been set up at a grade school near Harmon and Paradise Roads.

At 3:00 p.m. we were briefed on our assignments by the watch commander. My squad was chosen to go to the hotel and search for bodies, entering from the roof via helicopter. I was given an ax and a flashlight and was told that the gurneys were on-site.

The watch commander explained that the previous shifts had cleared the hotel from the casino to the 19th floor. We were to go in and clear from 19 to the penthouses on the 26th floor. The hotel room doors were supposed to be open — we were to use the axes to break in if the safety latches were on. At that, we all looked at each other. We knew that if the safeties were on, there were most likely dead bodies inside. Unless, of course, the guests had broken out the windows and jumped.

My ten-man squad boarded a police bus, en route to the chopper pad in the southeast parking lot that would serve as our staging area. Soon we would be searching and hoping to save lives. However, as we drove toward the blacked-out MGM, deep inside I knew the odds were stacked against us saving anyone.

In any event, I thought I was ready.

When we got to the parking lot, each squad member was handed two gurneys and told to board the helicopter. As we lifted off into the smoky twilight, the cold, horrid smell of death was all around us. It was an eerie feeling as I looked down at the dead Grand hotel among the glitter of its neighbors. From the sky it resembled a burned-out tenement in the middle of a large carnival.

We landed on the MGM rooftop, dimly lit by generated light. There I noticed several body bags lined up that were loaded onto the chopper after we got out. They would soon be headed to the grade school morgue.

A lieutenant pointed me in the direction of a rooftop door. As I entered the landing, balancing a gurney on each shoulder with a flashlight in one hand and an ax in the other, I heard a voice from the stairwell below say, "Go on down to 19."

I wasn't even sure how far that was, but I started walking. By the time I got there it seemed a lot farther than seven floors. When I got to the 19th floor, a fireman called out, "We need seven over here!"

I walked in his direction thinking, "Seven what? You mean there are seven dead people up here?" Sure enough, that was exactly what he meant.

He pointed me down the pitch-black hallway and said, "Go to the elevator and watch your step."

The gurneys were heavy as hell by then, and I nearly stumbled over the seven bodies lying in the hallway. I dropped the gurneys near the elevator and was handed a body bag. The corpses had to be tagged and bagged.

As I shined my flashlight down the hallway, it was like the scene of a bad horror movie or an episode from The Twilight Zone. I vividly remember the faces of the dead and the look of fear and horror in their eyes. Until that day I never knew that if you died in horror, your face actually stayed that way. I guess I'd never thought about it before.

One poor lady was wearing eyeglasses and the right lens was cracked like a spider web. She was completely gray and looked about my mom's age. I couldn't help but think that this was someone's mom. I knew I had to stop that thought or I wouldn't be able to go on.

We had been told in our briefing that day that several people had died in the stairwells as they tried to make it to the rooftop. One guy had died trying to shield his wife from the smoke, and they both just collapsed, with his arms wrapped around her. All of these deaths were from smoke inhalation, as the flames never made it up that far.

The squad we had just relieved had already placed toe tags on the victims lying in the hallway. Because the hotel records had burned, we attached some type of I.D. to each body. A wallet, credit card, or receipt; anything was good as long as it was bagged with the right person. That's when they paired us with partners, and mine was Officer Stubbs. We bagged the bodies, placed them on gurneys, and carried them back up to the rooftop.

Stubbs and I worked well together, as we were running on pure adrenaline in a mixed state of shock and disbelief. By this time we had worked our way up one floor, breaking down doors and searching for bodies with our flashlights. There I saw some of the saddest sights I have ever seen.

This one guy, about 55 years old, had thrown a chair through his window. In his dying mind's frenzy, he had ripped the curtains off the wall and tied them end to end to his bed sheets and pillowcases. He lay there, just inside his broken-out window, clutching his "escape rope" with both hands. I held back my tears, but it only got worse.

I remember Stubbs calling me from across the hall. He had found a young lady who'd died in her bathtub. She tried to survive by jamming wet towels under her doors to keep the smoke out. I gave Stubbs a hand lifting her out of the tub and placing her in a bag.

It was obvious that the smoke must have been unbelievable, as gray soot was everywhere. All of the dead people looked gray.

I recall carrying five or six people from the 20th floor, and a couple of people from 21 and 22. I was starting to relax a little, as the smoke seemed to have been thinner the higher up we went, so the people on the upper floors had probably made it to the rooftop. I had seen footage on TV earlier that day of people clinging to the helicopters and being brought to safety.

But there was this one room on the 24th or 25th floor I had to break into because the safety latch was still on. I cringed, knowing that this was not a good sign. As I entered the room and shined my flashlight across the bed, I jumped back a little and whispered, "My God!"

I got closer to the bed and pulled back the covers of a young couple who had died in their sleep. They were still locked in an embrace.

I had to stop for a minute to compose myself, as I knew I would soon be breaking them apart and putting them in bags. I shined my flashlight around the room and noticed her nightgown at the foot of the bed. On the dresser was a soot-covered bouquet of red roses and next to them was a large photo of this beautiful couple. Their poor families somewhere were worried about them, for sure. Now I was the first to confirm their deaths.

I picked up their picture and started to cry. I couldn't help it.

I remember thinking how nice it would be if I had one great big body bag, so I could put them in it together. After completing the hardest thing I had ever done in my life, I tried to pull myself together before I called down the hall for Stubbs.

We finally finished sweeping the penthouse suites, and luckily, all of those people had survived. I remember looking out of the penthouse windows on the Flamingo Road side of the building, and there were media trucks and satellite dishes as far as I could see. I swear every media outlet in the world was on Flamingo Road that night.

In fact, my folks back in Chicago called me the next day to say they saw me on TV on Nightline or something. I guess during the ordeal Stubbs and I had walked behind a live feed. They were seriously concerned about how I was doing. I lied and told them I was just fine. I figured there was really no need to make them worry; besides, I was a macho Las Vegas cop. If they only knew how many times over the years I have cried reliving that night.

It was nearly 5:00 in the morning when we were relieved and placed on security detail near the front doors of the once-opulent hotel. In those hotel rooms there was money, casino chips, and jewelry everywhere. If I were a thief, I could have retired the next day.

The casino had burned so fast I heard that people actually died with playing cards and drinks in their hands. It was like a fireball, they said. I just had to see it close up, so Stubbs and I used our coffee break to take a look around. We didn't know then, of course, that what we were witnessing would turn out to be the worst disaster in Nevada history.

It was eerie walking into the casino, now charred and dimly lit by generated light. I had stayed at the Grand several times before I'd even moved to Las Vegas. In fact, I'd dated a beautiful cocktail waitress from there and hoped to God she hadn't worked that morning. (I later found out that she hadn't.)

Stubbs and I walked up to the very craps table I had tried to learn the game on just a year before. It was burnt black, and I noticed the melted, soot-covered dice were still on the table. I also found a filthy MGM silver dollar at a blackjack table. I've kept these items over the years as sad mementos.

Finally, I just had to go the bar where I had my first drink in Vegas in the summer of '78. As I looked out over the casino floor, the scene was so surreal I had a hard time accepting the tragedy. My mind kept reverting back to the bright colors, gorgeous ornate chandeliers, happy smiling faces, bells, whistles, and action as far as the eye could see. That was the Vegas and MGM I loved. Hell, that was part of the reason I moved there from Chicago, and now it was all gone in a matter of minutes.

As I wondered, "What is God's message here?" I didn't even notice I was standing in six inches of water with my brand new boots on. I guess life had just taken on a new meaning for me; besides, I was like a zombie by then.

Every year at about this time I say a few prayers for all the families who lost loved ones that day. Over my nearly 30 years in law enforcement I've seen some sad and crazy things, but nothing affected me more than that one November night back in my rookie year.

BINGO!

One early morning at 3am, I was headed southbound on Maryland Parkway when I saw headlights coming right at me on my side of the road! I got out of the way, popped a U-turn, and gave chase to the car going down the wrong side of the road. He finally saw my flashing lights and pulled into a shopping center parking lot and stopped. I walked up to his car and the guy was obviously hammered.

"Officer I am so sorry, I miscalculated my left turn back there and all I wanna do is get home ... I was out with a buddy who is going through a bad divorce and I think I'm drunk!"

I appreciated this guy's honesty and noticed by his driver's license that he lived three or four blocks from where we were. I didn't have the heart to arrest the poor bastard, since he was so nice and respectful, and all I wanted to do was make sure nobody got hurt. His name was Tony.

"I tell you what, Tony. Let's lock up your car and I will give you a ride home." He couldn't believe I said that.

So I locked up his car, gave him my business card and wrote on the back where his car was parked, and drove him home. When we got up the stairs to his house he was so thankful, and then the door opened and his wife laid into him. He would have probably had a much more peaceful night if I locked him up, I thought to myself. They thanked me profusely; they both knew he was in the wrong and said it wouldn't happen again. She agreed not to get his car until later that day.

The next night after briefing I had a phone call at the back of the station. It was the drunk driver Tony from the night before crying on the phone how I saved his life and his job. He went on to tell me that he was the head guy at Caesar's Palace showroom and if I ever wanted to see a show it was on him for me and a guest. BINGO! I thought to myself.

Two weeks later, I saw the big marquee sign that Frank Sinatra was appearing at Caesar's Palace and my brother Cliff was coming to town to see me. Of course I immediately paid a visit to my new best friend, Tony! When he saw me he hugged me so hard he nearly broke my neck. He said, "You bring your brother to the front of the line Saturday night!"

Cliff and I were treated like royalty sitting in the first row – our food and drinks were comped by Tony. When I tried to tip him he pushed me away so I left money for the wait staff. What a night!

I guess sometimes when you treat people nice it comes back around.

I was dating this one camera girl from the Flamingo at the time and she wanted to see Diana Ross at Caesar's, so Tony took care of that, as well. We remained pretty good friends and I would always stop by to say hi whenever I was in the area. I really appreciated his kindness but just didn't want to burn him out.

Star Sightings

Living in Vegas, it's hard not to run into entertainers and other VIPs. Often times it happens when you least expect it.

I was having cocktails one night at the Tropicana Casino Bar when they were filming an episode of the hit series VEGAS, in which the late Robert Urich played Dan Tanna. I was watching the commotion of the film crew in the casino when one of the bartenders I knew said that she had gotten friendly with the director over the past few days and asked me if I wanted to be an "extra". I said "sure," as I had never been on TV before and I always watched that show.

During their break, the director came over to the bar with Urich and my friend introduced me to both men and told them that I was a METRO cop. They liked that, and asked me if I wanted to be in a scene out front where I would exit the revolving door and walk up to valet and hand them a ticket. Urich would soon follow me, and his red T-Bird was parked out front waiting for him. I handed the valet my ticket as Urich stood next to me and the valet flipped him his keys. He then pulled out of the area followed by the film crew and that was it. We only did two takes but it was pretty cool, and even cooler when my Ma and Dad saw me on TV back in Chicago.

One early morning I was finishing my reports in my squad car just before I got off shift. I was under a shade tree at 7:30 a.m., near the green for a par three at the Las Vegas Country Club. This was a ritzy neighborhood with nice big ranch style custom homes throughout. I saw the door open on the house across the street and one house down and out stepped Englebert Humperdinck in his bath robe with his hair all messed up. He was coming out to grab the morning paper from his lawn when he smiled and waved at me. I waved back and drove over to him to say "good morning." He was a big deal in the early 80s there on the Strip at The Aladdin. He walked over to my car and I noticed that his front door was wide open and I could see a swimming pool in his living room. We exchanged pleasantries and I asked him, "Is that a pool in your living room?"

He said, "Yes, would you like to see it?"

I said, "sure."

I followed him inside and saw that he had a lap pool right there in his living room, with a retractable roof and comfy beach chairs all around. He said that he loved to swim to stay in shape. He then offered me a cup of coffee and comped tickets to see his show. I turned down the coffee but made his day when I told him I had already seen his show twice. I explained that it seemed like every girl I dated wanted to see him perform! He said he liked that, and I then had to run. He was a really nice guy.

I was called to The Las Vegas Hilton early one evening to take a burglary report in one of the penthouse suites. I knocked on the door and one of the most beautiful women I had ever seen opened the door. I was somewhat stunned by her beauty as she invited me in. I couldn't help but notice the size of the penthouse and the panoramic view of Las Vegas. She said her name was Rhonda and that there was a large diamond ring missing from her bedroom. It was quite expensive, and she had a picture of it and paperwork with an appraised value of $4500. She said that she thought the cleaning crew did an inside job, but she didn't know when exactly it went missing because she had just noticed it was gone and called METRO.

All of the sudden, John Davidson walks into the room from the bedroom area and introduced himself. I had noticed his name on the Hilton Marquee when I pulled in. I told him what a beautiful room he had, and he said, "This is where Elvis stayed when he played here." I thought that was pretty cool.

He was very nice and he offered me a diet Coke as I took the burglary report. It turned out that Rhonda was one of his backup singers, and I assumed they were shacking up together but didn't ask as it was not my business. In any event, they made a nice couple and in fact got married. I think they still might be married.

I was called to Caesar's Palace for a room break in call, and as I walked around the corner in the casino I bumped into this little black guy and accidently knocked him down. I instinctively reached out my hand to help him up, saying I was sorry, and when I grabbed his hand I saw that he had all these gold and diamond rings on. Then I saw his gold chain and eyeglasses. It was Sammy Davis Jr. He profusely apologized to me, saying he wasn't watching where he was going. I cleaned him off and made sure he was OK. I was stunned to see that he was only about 5 feet tall and probably weighed 110 pounds. Bouncing off of me at 5 feet 11 and 215 pounds he went flying. I felt bad, but he was quite a nice man.

The actor Gianni Russo, who played in The Godfather and several other movies, had a bar and restaurant in Las Vegas on Sahara, which I frequented on my days off. It was a great place where all the pretty people hung out. Don't ask me why I was there. A lot of the entertainers and mobsters went in there and I saw the likes of Diana Ross, Donna Summer, Elton John, Larry Holmes, and of course Gianni himself, who was really a cool guy.

Thank God I'm a Good Guy!

I was driving eastbound on Tropicana near Maryland Parkway when a stabbing call came out at a bar across the street from UNLV. I knew the area pretty well, so I advised control that I had already arrived in the vicinity. When I pulled my squad car into the back lot of the bar, I could see a bunch of people in a chaotic state waiving their hands and pointing to the cars in the lot. I jumped out and heard somebody scream, "There he goes officer…Get him!"

I gave foot chase behind this Charlie Manson-looking dude with blood all over his face, long hair, and white T-shirt. He darted between the cars and I could see a shiny object in his right hand as I got closer. I advised control of the direction of my foot pursuit as I heard others from my squad say they had arrived.

I then saw him pitch the shiny object under a car as he kept running for his life.

That's when Officer Andy perfectly positioned his squad car and gunned it in front of our boy as he tried to cross the street. It was a thing of beauty as the guy hit the front quarter panel of Andy's squad car and flew over the hood, landing in the street where I could easily cuff him. I then patted him down and asked Andy for a lift back to my patrol car. Later, we laughed about it as I told him he was my new law enforcement idol. He helped make a great pinch and never got out of his car. "That's good police work if I ever saw it," I proclaimed. Andy just smiled.

I then had the homicide detectives join me as I needed to find and photograph whatever my collar threw down in the parking lot, and I wasn't sure if the stabbing victim would live. Of course Andy "supervised" the search again, all by sitting in his car and pointing in the general area where I told him the knife would be.

They found a bloody folding knife underneath one of the vehicles where I had seen the perp pitch it. The knife was given to me after it was photographed in place and bagged and tagged as evidence.

The ambulance attendants were working on the stabbing victim and they were unsure if he would make it or not. They told me, "He was ripped up pretty good."

I placed the bloody suspect in the front seat of my patrol car and had a few eye witnesses confirm that they had seen him do the stabbing. I then read him his Miranda Rights (verbatim) right off the card I had gotten from the academy. I didn't want to make any mistakes as I thought this might turn out to be a murder pinch.

As the paramedics loaded the victim into the ambulance, my suspect asked me, "What should I do now?"

I said, "If I were you, first I would say a prayer that the guy on that gurney over there doesn't die. Then I would start thinking about finding some money for a good lawyer." He just looked at me, very scared and rightly so.

As we drove downtown to central booking, we made small talk about life in Las Vegas. I asked him if he knew any good attorneys in town. He said that he didn't, but maybe his girlfriend did. I told him he could call her when we got to the jail. He then voluntarily told me about his girlfriend and why he had stabbed the guy at the club. "The guy gave her a bad time last night so I went there to get even." He explained.

"Jesus Christ, kid, I don't think you should be telling me this stuff," I said.

I then blurted..."And why didn't you just kick his ass? Did you have to bring a knife and stab him?"

Then there was silence.

I remember thinking to myself that his girlfriend must be one real hot piece of ass or he is the dumbest bastard on the planet. Probably a little bit of both!

"Let's talk about sports or something else if you wanna talk, okay?" I changed the subject.

When we pulled into the jail entry area, I again patted down and ran a cursory search on the suspect just as we had learned to do in the academy. I was let inside the outer cage area and placed my service gun and baton in the lockers and grabbed my key. The elevator doors opened and we got on. When we got off on the second floor, I walked my prisoner to the check in booking window, took off his handcuffs, and asked him to empty his pockets on the ledge. The intake officer behind the glass would inventory his belongings. I then asked him to remove his belt.

From behind his belt buckle he removed a small, pearl handled two-shot Derringer and placed it on the counter. I couldn't believe my eyes as my knees began to buckle. I instinctively moved my hand to cover or take control of my stupid fumble, but it was too late. The intake officer saw it and also saw my embarrassed, red face through the glass.

Luckily for me, the booking officer was a good guy. He told me to place it in evidence like I had taken it off of him in the street. The booking Sergeant never saw it, thank God!

I remember thinking how lucky I was that my arrestee didn't shoot me in the head as soon as I took off his handcuffs. I also wanted to crawl into a hole, as it was a really bad rookie mistake. I recall seeing a few training videos during our academy where the cops in the jails had their heads blown off just like that! Needless to say, from that night on I played more like a "proctologist" to every arrestee before I cuffed them and placed them in my squad car.

I then took my new friend and "prisoner of the year" into the room to be strip searched. That's when I asked him, "Why didn't you just kill me?"

His answer was, "Because you're a good guy!"

I immediately wanted to hug this crazy, blood soaked new friend of mine, but I didn't. All I could do was wish him well with his impending legal matter.

And as I drove the 15 minutes back to the Strip to go back in service, I thanked the Lord that my Mom and Dad back in Chicago had raised me right. There is no doubt that if I had disrespected this guy and treated him like shit, I would be a dead man.

I learned two very important lessons that night, and if you are a young police officer, perhaps you should listen:

Be sure to double search all your prisoners before placing them in your squad car.

Be nice to everyone you lock up. It doesn't cost anything and just might save your life in case you screw up.

The Peppermill Pinch

My 10-hour shift was only 20 minutes from ending when the dispatcher said, "2 King 12, copy a call ...a disturbance at the Peppermill."

Now, the call was actually assigned to day shift, but I was near The Peppermill and, being the eager rookie cop that I was, I jumped at the call and advised control, "1 King 2 arrived at The Peppermill, cancel 2 King 12."

As I pulled my black and white into the restaurant driveway, I saw a man in a shirt and tie waving his arms, directing me to the back parking lot. My window was rolled down, and he told me that he was the manager and there was a guy inside who was creating a disturbance.

"Last week this guy punched out one of my busboys, and my cook told me that he overheard a conversation that the guy was running from the police back east," the manager said.

I wasn't sure what I had, but I needed to be safe. Since I was in uniform, I called for two plain-clothed detectives to assist. Detectives Rose and Barlow stopped by, and I explained the situation. The manager let us in the back door and he pointed out the subject through the small rectangular window that separated the kitchen from the restaurant. He was a black-haired Italian-looking kid in a black leather jacket. Rose and Barlow were two old pros with about 35 years of combined experience, and they had no problem walking around the front as if they were going to buy a cup of coffee, surprise our boy, and escort him to the back lot for me. I watched through the small window as they astonished the young man and safely escorted him to the back lot and in front of my patrol car. I have to admit that I didn't know these two detectives from Adam, and I was somewhat intimidated by their presence as I began my questioning after I had patted him down. First, I asked for some I.D. and the kid said he didn't have any.

"Empty your pockets on the hood of my car," I said politely.

As he began reaching in his pants pockets, I asked him his name.

"Johnny. Why?" he asked, as he dropped 18 cents on the hood of my patrol car.

That was all he had on him.

"Johnny what?" I asked in my sarcastic tone.

"Lorenzo. Why?"

I then asked this Johnny Lorenzo character how he planned to pay for the 35 cent cup of coffee he was drinking. He just shrugged. I then noticed some familiar jailhouse tattoos on his arms, and as he stood in the sunlight, I could see his hair was dyed black. The blonde roots gave it away.

I asked Johnny if he had ever been arrested before in Las Vegas, and he replied, "Yeah, once."

"Would you care to elaborate for me?" I asked.

"I got popped pissin' in a stairwell at the airport about 10 days ago. Why?"

This guy and his whys and his back east accent! Something just wasn't sitting right with me.

I ran him on my squad car computer and sure enough, Johnny Lorenzo was arrested 10 days ago at McCarran Airport for pissin' in public.

Now, it was getting late, so Rose and Barlow pulled me aside and said, "Hey kid, this is going nowhere fast."

That's when I made my first really bad rookie mistake. I told them I wanted to book this guy on something because I just didn't feel right. I should have just let those guys leave, 'cause they both thought I was another green, hot-shot rookie bordering on stupidity.

I said, "Maybe I could book him for defrauding an innkeeper? He only had 18 cents, you know?"

Rose and Barlow looked at me as if I had two heads and said, "See you later, kid; it's your call."

I thanked them for the hand and told them I owed them a cup of coffee. Talk about peer pressure! Anyway, I wasn't satisfied, but I knew I would look like a real fool if my gut wasn't right. I asked the manager to get the cook who overheard Johnny say he was running from trouble back east somewhere.

I spoke broken Spanish to Juan, the cook, and he told me that his wife had overheard Johnny talking on the phone saying that he couldn't go back to Miami. I thought it was strange that Johnny was staying with Juan and his wife, so I asked the cook to explain.

"He's a friend of my wife's brother," the cook said. He only knew him as Johnny.

I then asked the Peppermill manager if he would do me a favor. I needed him to follow me and Johnny downtown. I needed him to file a complaint against Johnny for defrauding an Innkeeper. Now, even the manager thought I was nuts, but I explained that I didn't feel right letting this guy "walk" since he had no I.D. and no money, and he had dyed hair and jailhouse tattoos, and besides, he might have been on the run. And I wasn't certain he was Johnny Lorenzo.

The manager followed me downtown and I put Johnny into a holding cell after I explained to the booking officer that I was headed to the fugitive squad to try and get a detainer. I knew it was definitely a long shot, but I made my way to Sergeant Jules Goldberg's office. He ran the fugitive squad. I had never met the silver-haired sergeant before, but when he swiveled in his chair, unlit cigar in his mouth, his experienced demeanor caused me to smile.

"Whatcha got, kid?"

I started my dissertation with the opening line, "Sarge, I'm really not crazy."

He motioned with his right hand as if to say, "Keep talking."

So I did. I could tell he wasn't all that enthused, so I asked him if I could make a call because I wanted to follow-up on a conversation the cook's wife had overheard. He smiled and pointed to another room where I could use a phone. I dialed the home number the cook gave me, and a female with a Hispanic accent answered. I asked for Juan. She said Juan hadn't gotten home from work yet. I really hoped she was Juan's wife. I asked her about the phone conversation she had overheard between Johnny Lorenzo and someone.

She said, "Not Johnny Lorenzo. Johnny Lorenzo is my brother."

I said Johnny was with me, when it finally dawned on me. I asked her to describe her brother, and she said he was about 6'2" with brown hair and a mustache. I knew the Johnny I had in the cage was only about 5'9". I asked her if her brother had any tattoos, and when she said "No," I wanted to crawl through the phone cord and give her a hug. She said she overheard the conversation between her brother's friend she only knew as Frankie and someone else. She heard him saying he was running from Miami and he couldn't go back there.

It was all finally starting to make sense. This guy who was caught pissin' in the stairwell 10 days prior was booked as Johnny Lorenzo alright, but he wasn't really Johnny Lorenzo. That much I knew for sure. Now if I could only convince Goldberg.

I went back to his office and, based on my new revelation, he agreed to sit in on my interview with Johnny (who we now believed to be Frankie). I thought going in that if I could get this Frankie character to tell the good old Sergeant to go fuck himself, I would be on my way. I felt that Frankie was certainly capable of that. I played the experience factor with Goldberg and he ate it up. I felt confident that these two would not mesh. Frankie sat down and before I could say a word, the Sergeant took a crack at his old technique. It was beautiful to watch.

Franky screamed, "Fuck you! I want an attorney."

Goldberg looked at me, got up, and said, "Let's go kid."

I had my 72-hour detainer. I will never forget the look on Frankie's face as I said through the bars, "I'm not sure who you are, but I know who you are not."

We went back to Goldberg's office, and he alluded that he was an ex-New York copper and he knew the drill. I said, "Let's pull a few strings, and get these prints classified and to Miami PD."

He just smiled and assured me he'd do what he could do. We shook hands and I went back to my locker at the south substation, hoping that Rose and Barlow would keep their mouths shut if I was wrong. Talk about a long shot!

I went home that morning after three hours of overtime and I hit the pillow at 11:30 a.m. I had just fallen asleep when the phone rang.

"Hello?" I said.

"Rusin?" The voice sounded familiar.

"Yeah, who's this?" I asked.

"Bingo," said the voice.

"Who's this?" I asked again.

"Goldberg. You did it, kid. BINGO!"

I knew this had to be good as I sat up on the edge of my bed. Goldberg told me that the wise guy was Francis "Frankie" Fragoso, and he had killed his 19-year old girlfriend in the south beach section of Miami. "Stabbed her real good and then choked her with a lamp cord." Sarge said.

The hairs on my arms stood straight up.

"Miami PD is elated, and they're on their way to extradite this puke," Goldberg continued. "Just beeyutyfull, kid... You did it!"

I was so happy that I couldn't sleep. I looked forward to seeing Rose and Barlow that night. In fact, moments after I logged on, they asked for a meet at the local 7-11. Those guys were real class acts as they congratulated me and thanked me for showing them a few things. I told them I'd like to buy them that cup of coffee I promised, but they insisted that it was on them. And as we sipped away, we all knew that I had finally earned the right to call myself a cop.

Note: This pinch earned me a letter of commendation that my great Sergeant Keaton sent up my chain of command. It also gained me instant respect from my peers and bosses. Word spread through the department like wildfire and it made me feel great. It was like hitting the lottery!

A Hot Vegas Night

I recall the way my 10-hour shift began back on that hot summer night in 1981. The memory is as vivid as it can be. We called it the "graveyard" shift because it was known to be dead in most towns in America between 10:00 p.m. and 8:00 a.m. But, this was no ordinary town; this was Las Vegas where things stayed hot all night long. Hell, that's why I'd moved to Sin City, and that's why I was dressed in my cool summer short-sleeved shirt.

You see, I was a member of the toughest street gang in the state of Nevada. I was one of Las Vegas' finest. We were known as "METRO," aka: the Las Vegas Metropolitan Police Department. Even our badges were cool!

It was the same old briefing at 10:00 p.m. sharp and the same old "hot sheets" with the wanted persons and stolen cars made it a seemingly routine start. I logged onto my unit as "1 John 12", checked my vehicle, and rolled out of the South Substation at around 10:30 p.m. I was expecting it to be just another night on the streets, but you can never be too sure.

No sooner did I go in service, when the dispatcher greeted me with "1 John 12, copy a call."

I had a few calls backed up, as usual, and for a Thursday night that wasn't too bad. My first was a domestic disturbance and my backup "1 John" was rolling my way, but I just happened to be closer to the call. I wondered what was going on as I made my way to the given address.

I pulled up and could hear a female's screams from the street. Training kicked in right away. I knew I was supposed to wait for my backup, but 1 John was only a few blocks away. He'd make it there in time, I thought to myself. As I approached the screen door, I could see a man beating a screaming, crying female as he straddled her on the front room couch. "Shit," I muttered.

I knew I had to stop the beating. I entered the room and yelled at the man, "POLICE! Stop!"

He turned around for a second and muttered, "Fuck you, asshole!" or something to that effect as he continued to beat away as though I wasn't even there.

I took a step back and calmly asked 1 John for his ETA, and he replied, "1 John arrived."

I then saw that the lady's face was all bloody and beaten to shit. As 1 John entered the front door we knew we had no choice. I was behind the bully and my thoughts were to get this guy stopped and handcuffed without him getting my gun. "Gun retention," I said to myself.

I hit the guy high and 1 John hit him low, and the fight was on. We had to get him cuffed, and as the two of us tried rolling him over, I saw the lady get off the couch. I started to scream, "Hey, get back here!" when she disappeared around the corner muttering a few words to herself. Now I had one eye on the asshole, trying to help 1 John cuff him and one eye on the corner where the lady went.

The apartment was rather small and located on the second floor. There was a sliding glass door leading to the balcony, and the place had a weird, funky vibe to it. Needless to say, I did not want to be there.

We almost had the cuffs on the asshole when this crazed, screaming bloody lady came running around the corner with a butcher knife raised above her head. I screamed, "Mike (aka 1 John)!"

Then I just snapped and I don't know where I got my strength. I tackled the goofy bitch and ran her ass out through the sliding glass door. The balcony railing probably saved her life, because I went into her with the full force of my body. Glass was everywhere, and all I could do was think about what a nut I was for trying to help this lady out. I knew this cop stuff was a thankless job, but come on! Coming at me with a butcher knife after I stopped her face from being caved in?

Needless to say, Mr. and Mrs. Asshole both went to jail and, as luck would have it, they were married, so obviously she refused to press charges. Ultimately, I booked her with "Assault with a Deadly Weapon on a Police Officer" and that was that.

After my trip downtown, I remember driving by the bank at Maryland Parkway and Twain. The digital sign at the bank read 12:15 a.m. and the temperature was 100 degrees. I mean, it was midnight, pitch black out and it was still 100! Little did I know that it was about to get hotter!

The shrill beep alerted all the patrol cars on the west side of town, letting us know that a guy had just been shot in the neck and dumped from his vehicle onto the street. I recall sitting behind the Circle K and meeting 1 John, laughing about our earlier scrape when I went to channel 5 on the radio to attempt to run the registration on the vehicle involved, but my fellow "Metrons" had beaten me to it. I figured that if the guy was shot and dumped from his car, the keys to his house were probably on the same key ring as those to his car. Everyone I know carries their vehicle registration in their glove box.

Now I'm no Dan Tanna (detective from the show Vegas in the 1970s), but I was hoping the guy's house wasn't too far from my beat. It was just a hunch. When I heard the dispatcher say "1979 black Rivera" and "Mark Twain Apartments," Mike and I smiled at each other and started rolling that way. As luck would have it, this was our turf.

As I drove toward the Mark Twain Apartments, I thought, this guy couldn't be this dumb. No sooner did I finish that thought when I heard Officer Willy say, "Control, what was the plate on that black Riviera?" Willy was westbound on Desert Inn, approaching Maryland Parkway. I said to myself, "Damn, Willy," as I flipped on my red lights to blow a stop sign or two.

The dispatcher repeated the plate number, and next thing Willy said was "code red." If a cop calls "code red," he is involved in a very dangerous situation and all other non-emergency radio traffic is halted. All units instinctively and quietly started rolling that way. In other words, it was show time!

Mike was right behind me as we approached Officer Willy in the street with his shotgun pointed at some guy lying near the curb behind the black Riviera. The Riviera was parked in the middle of

Desert Inn with both doors wide open, and I could see another guy running through the desert towards the wall to the Las Vegas Country Club far off in the distance.

I hollered at Mike and Willy, "I got him!"

Willy covered me as I walked up to pat down and handcuff one of the boys. Mike gave chase to the other guy as he hopped the seven-foot wall like it was nothing. I took a six-shot revolver from the punk's waistband and cuffed him. I opened the cylinder and found that one round had been spent. Willy walked up to clear the Riviera, and saw blood all over the driver's headrest, seat, and door.

I asked the guy I had nabbed a few questions, and he was either hard of hearing or he just didn't like me. I had him face down and cuffed, so I pulled his head back about 18 inches from the pavement and I said in my tough guy voice, "If you don't tell me who your partner is, and if he has a gun, I will bounce your head on the curb."

Thankfully, this guy bought it and he told me his partner's name and that he was armed with a six-shot revolver.

I immediately put this fact out on the air, as it was probably true and officer safety is number one. The detectives then showed up and I turned my guy and his gun over to them as Willy and I had to go help Mike and the others look for the other punk.

The Las Vegas Country Club had an entrance on Maryland Parkway, and squads were rolling that way. No cops tried to scale the wall because it was not safe. We had to wait. Then T.D. came screaming on the code red radio, "Shots fired…shots fired inside the Country Club!"

I could hear his car crash and then there was silence. Talk about adrenaline! My thoughts flashed from "I hope T.D.'s not dead" to "I want to kill this punk bastard."

This is where adrenaline takes over your body and all those training sessions that you undertake prove their value. I had to keep my thoughts straight.

I mean, I tried not to take it personally, but here was a guy trying to kill a cop and I was one. I rolled into the Country Club and was stationed by the Sergeant to a corner of the building near where the shooter had last been seen. Willy, who had a shotgun, was around the same corner, and Scott and Gary had the other corner. This guy was fair game and you could feel it in the air.

The chopper units now lit up the perimeter, and the Lieutenant decided to bring in the hounds. I stood there with my gun in my hand, trying not to get shot by this stranger. I looked left and right and prayed that he didn't pop out of the bushes and shoot me before I could shoot him. We all knew that he had just tried to kill a cop. What were the odds he was going to give up now?

I stood there during the longest hour of my life keeping as small and still as I could be. I was glad I had worn my bulletproof vest. There was a whirlwind going on in my head. I thought about God as my life flashed before me. I remember thinking about how sad my Ma and Dad would be if this guy killed me.

At that moment, I wished my whole family was there, because that way if I got shot, maybe they could come see me before I died. I thought about how I wanted to be buried in Chicago. Man, I should have been a fireman. At least I would die doing what I loved. This was all crazy stuff. Talk about adrenaline pumping. I just knew that I really didn't want to die there.

It took a while to get the beautiful Canine Corps geared up. For anyone who has never seen them in action, it's pretty amazing stuff. They picked up the scent of the perp at the Riviera and followed it over the wall as the squad cars were used to boost the dogs and their handlers. Once inside the Country Club, I could hear them in the distance, and it was music to my ears. Man, you could tell they were on it. As they came within 100 yards of the courtyard, the tension was elevated and it grew higher with every growling step.

I looked to my left then back again to my right as 4 bushes were in the courtyard in front of me. Left again, then right. Left again, then right, then bam, bam, bam, from my left I saw a muzzle flash from above a bush about 40 feet away. Instantly, I ducked and recoiled my body away from the muzzle flash threat. The dogs lunged for our guy as I could hear the rounds hit the stucco wall just above my head and felt remnants of the stucco chips and dust raining down on my head and shoulders.

I then heard the loudest shotgun I had ever heard ring out from my left side, and handguns rang out like popcorn in the night. I saw something go flying from the bushes as the dogs lunged for the shooter.

It all happened so fast! It was over within a couple of seconds. I never got a round off, and I was pissed. To this day, I am still pissed at what happened. The shots rang out so close to me that they were inches from my head. Until that night, I did not know for sure if I could kill someone if I had to. That night, I honestly could have killed that guy. No problem. I guess it was because he tried to kill T.D., who had on the same uniform and badge as I did. And then he tried to kill me!

When the gun battle stopped and the dogs had been taken away, we found out that our guy had been shot eight times, and amazingly he was still breathing. Then, we walked up to him and Officer

Gary pulled his head back by his hair and stuck his handgun in his mouth as if to execute the "scumbag".

I looked up and said, "Gary, NO!" as I noticed a lady standing on her balcony watching the commotion. Gary removed his gun from the asshole's mouth and walked away.

I then realized that the punk's right arm had been severed at the elbow; completely blown off and lying a few feet away. This was obviously a shotgun wound. I heard a few "attaboys" for Officer Willy, who had wielded the shotgun. The dogs had chewed on the punk's severed knee a bit, but it wasn't until he got to the hospital that he lost that appendage, as well. His gun was found under his fallen body with all six rounds spent. Unfortunately, he was still breathing.

I started to take a sigh of relief, but I still had to know about T.D. I looked past the ambulance hood and there he was, smiling like a big dog, just happy to still be alive. I walked up to him and hugged him and kissed his cheek. He knew what I meant.

As for the detective work, it turned out that the guy who we ended up shooting was hitchhiking when the poor victim picked him up in his black Riviera. Our guy shot the Riviera driver and dumped him for dead.

He then went to pick up his buddy, who was the first guy I "interrogated" at the curb. Our guy also gave the curb guy the gun he had just used to shoot the Riviera driver. They were on their way to burglarize the fancy Mark Twain Apartment since they knew nobody would be home, at least not the man of the house. However, due to some aggressive police work…they never made it.

It turned out that the driver of the Riviera had lived, but was paralyzed for the rest of his life, and so for all practical purposes, he was considered dead. Our "curb guy" testified on our side and our one-armed, one-legged man got an 80-year sentence.

As for that scene with the gun in the mouth, I later asked Officer Gary if he would have done it if I didn't scream at him. He said, "Nah, I just wanted to scare him a little."

And, if you're wondering if I would have bounced that kid's head on the pavement if he hadn't come around or if I only said no to the execution because I saw a witness, the answer is no on both counts.

I went back to the shooting scene the next afternoon as I wanted to see it in daylight. Actually, I wanted to see the spot where I could have easily died.

I crouched down where I was the night before and couldn't squeeze my body or head down lower than where the bullets hit, no matter how hard I tried. I was pleasantly perplexed. I then walked over to behind the bush and blood soaked grass where the suspect was shot to try and see his perspective as to where I was and how he missed me. With tears in my eyes I thanked God he was a shitty shot!

Then all of a sudden I heard an older female voice from her balcony, "You're partner should have blown his head off!" It was the same lady I had seen the night before on her balcony. "Thank you ma'am," was all I could say.

NOTE: The fact that I never returned fire that night bothered me. I was also worried that my partners might think that I was a coward or pussy.

I then tracked down the department shrink at our police bar and "off the record" he explained that because of the threat, surprise muzzle flash, and my body's automatic reaction, it was reasonable that I was not capable of returning fire even though I had wanted to. He also explained how my body was able to recoil so small that the shots went over my head by inches. When you are in fear of your life your body can do amazing things, he opined. That was good enough for me.

Jewel Heist at The Trop!

I was conducting a bar check at a loud topless joint south on Las Vegas Boulevard with my partner Gary when a theft call came out at the Tropicana Hotel. There was a bunch of commotion going on near the stage as I started to look for Gary in the crowd to let him know I would be leaving for The Trop. It was a wet T-shirt contest and crazy Gary was on stage (in uniform) with a spray bottle wetting down the dancers in their T-shirts! I just shook my head and pointed to my hand-held radio and waved goodbye. Gary was a crazy bastard and ex-New York copper which explains it all and probably why I loved that guy!

Upon my arrival at the Trop a fancy jewelry store name Le Bijou there off the casino that had just gotten ripped off in a rather well orchestrated, expensive wrist watch heist.

The two ladies who were working the store looked sick to their stomachs. I also was told by security that the owner, Michael, was on his way.

The ladies' stories seemed plausible; as the first thing that crossed my mind was that it was an inside job. They were too shaken up to have been a part of this and rather embarrassed that it had happened on their "watch". When I asked them if they would submit to polygraph tests, they both answered "yes" and that quickly ended any academy award presentations (I thought to myself).

The ladies explained that at approximately 6:30 p.m., about 25 Asians flooded the store and surrounded the center rectangular glass case. They blocked their views and made a distracting commotion, asking the ladies to show them some rings and things in a few side cases around the store. They had done such a good job that the ladies hadn't noticed anything other than commotion with a foreign language they did not understand. All of the sudden, the Asians all quickly left the store and jumped into cabs in the valet area. Just like that they were all gone.

Of course nobody bought anything, and when one of the ladies grabbed the Windex bottle and towel to clean the Piaget watch case she noticed it was almost completely empty. She then blurted, "Oh my God...call security...we've been robbed!"

The thieves had used two screwdrivers to pry the rectangular glass from the wooden casing and then slid the glass enough to get their hands inside the case. All told, 21 Piaget diamond watches were stolen at roughly $10,000 a copy. They also took a few gold coins and some rings. The total amount they had gotten from the heist was worth $300,000.

These thieves were so good that they even brought wet wipes to wipe the case down to try and remove any fingerprints they may have left behind. The case was not alarmed and there was no video inside the store at that time. In other words, they did their homework!

The only good thing that came of this was that the owner Michael was a great guy who, with his lady friend, owned jewelry stores there in the Trop, the MGM Grand, and the Hilton. His son Danny and I became pretty good friends.

Michael was a big supplier from Los Angeles with his offices on Wilshire Boulevard. He took my advice to install cameras, alarm the cases, and hire a security guard. I also warned him not to drive around town alone with a half million dollars worth of diamonds, gold, and watches in his briefcase.

However, he would not take my warning to heart.

I learned a couple years later he was set up, robbed, and nearly killed in L.A.

He explained that the sting had gone like this: Some guy named Robert called him stating that he was opening a jewelry store in L.A. and needed some items to get started. Crazy Michael took his fancy Mercedes Benz and briefcase loaded with his stuff to meet with Robert. Michael left the briefcase in the trunk when he pulled up to the front of a jewelry store, which was being painted by two guys wearing painting gloves. Michael walked up to them and asked if this was Robert's new jewelry store. The men said yes, that Robert was in the back installing security cameras. "Just go back there in the back door...He's expecting you," they said.

Michael thought this was all good so he went to the back door where it was half opened and called for Robert. Some guy answers, "Michael? Yeah, come on in."

Michael entered and was immediately grabbed and knocked to the ground. His glasses flew off and a sheet was placed over his head as he was duct taped to a large heating pipe. They grabbed his car keys and that was that.

The car was found later that day engulfed in flames in some parking lot, and of course Michael's briefcase was missing.

The police found out that the rent had been paid with cash; the painters were a ruse and in on it, and no leads were left to go on. In the end, Michael was just happy to be alive. Again, the thieves did their homework and nobody really got hurt too badly. All in all a pretty good scam, I must admit!

The Real Pimps of Caesar's Palace

Some street whore named Candy, who I had cultivated as a snitch, said that she had had enough of the Caesar's Palace shakedowns. She confided in me that security would approach the girls sitting at the Cleopatra's Barge Bar and put the arm on them for a fifty dollar bill every night. The girls who wouldn't pay would get swooped up and cited for trespassing, as METRO would then be called to respond and take them to jail. I figured 50 whores times $50 was not a bad split for the security detail there every day of the year.

It was information worth looking into, and I was just the officer to do that. It all started to make sense why security wanted us to come in through the back loading dock when we would respond. Not me. I would park my squad car by the main entrance by the big fountains and stroll past the barge. I would point to the working girls as I walked by and took them all with me to the security office where they had the one girl in custody that wouldn't play their game. Now all the girls were going downtown, and it created quite a stir as my plan was working. They had already paid off security to sit there, but security couldn't protect them when METRO swooped in!

Candy was so pissed off that she agreed to wear a wire. I was so happy, and couldn't wait to tell my Sarge about my plan.

I asked for a meet, and when the Sarge pulled next to me I said, "Sarge I got a street hoe who agreed to wear a wire into Caesar's and record their extortion attempt."

He looked at me and said, "Have you lost your mind? Are you not aware that the Sheriff golfs with the Chief of Security at Caesar's?"

I blurted out, "Who gives a fuck?"

He blurted back, "I give a fuck! And if you like your job, I suggest that you give a fuck, as well.

"Now that you put it that way, okay, but I don't like the fact that these jagoffs squeeze these broads for cash, and when they don't pay they call us to enforce the laws...It's bullshit Sarge, and you know it," I responded.

He then shook his head and said, "If I were you I'd just drop it."

He then drove away. I sat there for a minute thinking to myself that my Dad was right; it's all bullshit! So much for my brilliant enforcement idea.

Needless to say, this soured me with security at Caesar's Palace and I started to hate getting calls there. These fat asses were a bunch of thieves and I avoided that place unless I had to respond.

Officially Suicide – 1 BIG Jagoff!

It was almost quitting time, and my partner Gary and I were sipping our morning coffee at The Village Pub. We were both looking forward to our next three days off when the dispatcher stated, "All units be aware of an emergency call of a 419 (dead body) behind The Village Pub."

I spit out my coffee and answered my portable radio "1 John and 1 John 2 arrived."

We both got up and walked out the back door, and in the early sunlight we saw a lady waving her arms frantically. Next to her was a young boy about 10 years old and a dog on a leash he was holding.

"Officer...Officer there's a dead guy hanging from a tree over there!" She pointed to a clump of trees in the desert about 100 yards from where we were standing and stated, "It looks like he was stabbed and hung!"

Gary chimed in, "Oh yeah, how old about and what color is the dead guy?"

"He looked white and young; about 20 I'd say. My boy was walking the dog and he saw him and came home and told me about it."

She said she lived in the apartments that were close by on Harmon Avenue. I asked the kid how he was doing and he seemed fine but did say he was "a little freaked out."

I got her name, address, and phone number as Gary went to get his squad car. I then petted the dog and asked the kid his dog's name to try and get the kid's mind back to normal.

"Pepper," he said. I then told them thanks and we'd take it from there.

I got in Gary's car and we rolled slowly to the clump of trees. All Gary said was, "Good thing he's white!"

I responded, "No shit. That's all we need is a black guy hanging in a tree just off the Strip."

When we got about 15 yards from the tallest tree we saw the body hanging and a steak of blood along his right breast bone. From a distance it looked like his right breast had been sliced. At closer look, his nose had bled out on his chest, probably because of the rope around his neck. He was shirtless, wearing black nylon pants pulled down below his dick and black high top converse gym shoes. They were definitely Chuck Taylors.

It looked like this kid had been living in this clump of trees in the desert. There was a recliner chair, a mattress, a pillow, and Playboy books everywhere. It was like a shady cove. Gary asked, "Does he have cable TV in here?" as he leafed through a Playboy book taken off the recliner chair.

Of course my answer was, "He did."

"I better call the Sarge and a couple detectives," I told Gary. "I'm sure "Slim" would like to see some of these books." That is what we called our beloved Sarge: Slim.

We just taped off the scene after we checked and confirmed he was dead and held it until the detectives arrived. It could have been a staged murder, but not likely. We still had to treat it as such until the coroner and detectives arrived.

The fat Sarge finally pulled up and asked, "Whadya got?"

"A dead white guy about 20 hanging from a tree. Looks like he accidentally hung himself while jerking off," I replied.

"Haw haw haw…I read about this shit!" The Sarge got out of his car to take a closer look.

"Do you want us to cut him down?" I asked.

"Nah, fuck him…let the dicks handle this. Haw haw haw! See that rope there hanging next to his head? Well, when he was jerking off he tried to grab that rope but missed and he accidentally sevened out," he said. ("Sevened out" is a craps term for when a seven is rolled after you have established a point and you lose your bet.)

"I don't get it, Sarge," I said. "What ever happened to just some good old fashioned jerking off?"

"Haw haw haw," Gary chimed in, "Sarge you are one sick bastard." He just laughed harder.

At our next briefing, Gary and I told the story in front of the squad. We explained how the Sarge knew all about this little jerking off maneuver and he tried to tell us that he had "read about it in a book!"

"Sure, Sarge…in a book!" I chimed in. The guys all laughed and the Sarge just howled…Haw haw haw!

Accident My Ass!

A stabbing call came out and I was the first to arrive at the second floor apartment. This white guy calmly came to the door and let me in. He turned and started walking away as if to lead me to the victim when he stopped just short of the kitchen. My tunnel vision and keen observations were looking for blood, somebody screaming in pain, or some normal sign of chaos at a typical stabbing scene, but it was all calm and there was no blood. Then he turned and faced me and I couldn't believe my eyes. He had the large handle of a knife sticking straight out of his chest.

"Jesus Christ," I blurted as my knees weakened and I slowly walked him over to his couch while I was simultaneously requesting paramedics to my location. I mean, this guy was as cool as a cucumber and I was more shaken up than him. I laid him on his back on his living room couch and told him not to move. I asked, "What the hell happened?"

"I was eating an apple and I tripped over the coffee table."

I looked around the floor but couldn't find an apple or an apple core or anything. I knew the kid was full of shit but just couldn't bring myself to scold him at this critical moment. Did this poor kid try and off himself? He seemed so normal and clean.

The paramedics hustled in and taped the knife handle in place, trying not to move it before they could get to the ER. His vital signs were still normal. I locked up the apartment after I checked the fridge to see if he had any apples. There were none. I also checked the garbage can to see if he might have had the last apple and perhaps there was a plastic bag in the trash. There was none. Lastly, I double checked the entire area around the coffee table again. No apple evidence. Now I was sure he was full of shit.

On my ride to the hospital I was deep in thought. What would compel a 23 year old kid to try and kill himself by plunging a knife into his chest? He seemed so normal. I really didn't want to hurt this kid if this was his cry for help. I knew I had to write a report.

They got the knife out of his chest and the doctor came out to show me the X- ray. The blade was in so deep it was only a half inch from coming out his back. "This is one lucky kid," the doctor opined. "Miraculously, no vital organs were damaged and the kid will be just fine."

I asked if I could talk to the kid and he said, "Sure."

When the kid saw me, he knew I knew. I then asked the nurses to leave the room and give me a few minutes. I didn't want any witnesses. I told him I would make him a deal if he would be honest. He started to cry and said he just got dumped by his girlfriend and recently lost his job. He couldn't take it so he knelt down and plunged the knife into his chest.

In my brilliant psychiatrist minded voice I blurted, "Are you crazy? You are a nice, good looking kid with your whole future in front of you. I don't know if you noticed but there is more fine pussy in this town per square foot than anywhere in America. I can help you find a better job and to hell with your old girlfriend!"

The kid just looked at me. I went on ... "I will write this report up just like you told me, that it was an accident, if you promise me right now that you will never do anything this crazy ever again."

I just couldn't see an attempted suicide mark on his record. Anyway, the kid took the deal and that was that.

The End Begins...Leaving Las Vegas!

I had just cleared a bar disturbance call and was driving alone northbound down Paradise Road just north of Desert Inn when a car sped by me. He was going so fast I figured he was an unmarked unit. No sane person would blow by a marked squad car like that, I thought. I sped up as I did not recognize the car as one of ours.

I advised dispatch that I was making a traffic stop and gave her the license plate info of the speeder. I didn't have a radar gun but I surmised he was going at least 60 in a 40 mph zone. I had to go 70 mph just to catch up to him.

As I walked up on the driver, I was surprised to learn he did not identify himself as on off duty copper. No, he said, he was visiting from Chicago. I asked to see his driver's license as he explained it was a Hertz rental car he was in. Dispatch confirmed that fact.

He handed me an Illinois driver's license with a crisp $50 bill folded in fours behind it.

I immediately said, "Excuse me sir, but this bill must have stuck to your license by accident." I handed the bill back to him as he just grinned.

"Sir, you were going at least 60 mph and I don't know if you saw me or not, but I would like to hope you didn't."

"No sir, I didn't see you…I'm not that crazy," he blurted back.

After running him through the system he came back clean, so I decided to just give him a verbal warning. He seemed honest and cooperative, and besides, he was from my home town. I warned him also to be careful as, "This is not Chicago!"

He knew what I meant, thanked me and that was that... Or so I thought.

About a month later, I was at City Hall and across the pavilion I saw the same guy that was driving the speeding rental car. I didn't let him see me, but my head was spinning. He had said that he was a visitor from Chicago. Visitor my ass, I thought to myself. I then saw a "brass" I knew and asked him who that guy was as I pointed to him. He's on the "rat squad" was his answer. In other words, Internal Affairs. My head spun some more. My thoughts ranged from "thank God my parents raised me right" to "these bastards tried to set me up". I guess they were hoping I would have kept the $50. This sickened me.

I was thinking that they were after me because I had wanted the street whore to wear a wire into Caesar's Palace and get the security guards there who were shaking down the whores to work Cleopatra's Barge.

Or was it the fat ass Lieutenant who warned me to stay out of the mobbed up Tower of Pizza only to witness him frequenting the joint himself, both on and off duty?

I was still bitter that they had made me take a polygraph test regarding that slime ball who had said that I sold him guns from our METRO vault.

Either way, by the spring of 1983, I began to be disillusioned with the job.

Then I made a really bad mistake at Caesar's Palace. They had again called us to transport a whore for trespassing. This simply means she wouldn't pay security the $50 "extortion money" to let her sit there. They had her in a security room and her small hand purse was dumped out in front of her on the desk.

I walked in and knew exactly what had happened, but I had to act like their arrest was legit. The security officer said it looked like she had two pills in her purse. I didn't recognize either pill. They wanted me to add the charge for possession of a controlled substance to her arrest. I wasn't sure it was lawfully obtained so I dropped the pills in my coffee cup and when they fizzed up I said, "These aren't narcotics." A very dumb move on my part, but I was disgusted to have to play enforcer for their bullshit scam. I had done it for some time by then.

In any event, they beefed me for that and I did a day off without pay for destroying possible evidence. I was also transferred off the Strip and would now report to the west substation.

Luckily for me, ATF started hiring special agents in the summer of 1983. I had my degree and street experience, and in my heart it was time for a change. One summer day I saw the vacancy announcement posted on the board and decided to drive down to the Vegas Federal building and inquire about an application and look into the hiring process. When I walked into the ATF office, I was greeted by a really cool agent named John. Although I had on gym shorts, a tank top and flip flops he knew I was a METRO man and he said, "Don't worry about it. As soon as he gets off the phone I want you to meet the boss."

I shot back, "John, are you crazy? I just stopped in for an application not a friggin' interview. I'm not dressed. Don't do this to me!"

He said, "Come on in. Don't worry about it." John made me feel great!

We walked into the big office and Mike was the boss. He was another cool cat. We all sat down and for about an hour they grilled me on what I was doing on the job. There was a serial rapist running around Vegas for a week, and I was assigned to the undercover squad to try and catch the bastard. We also talked about the MGM Grand Hotel fire that John and I had worked back in 1980. I pulled dead bodies out as a cop, and John was with ATF on the investigative team.

He took me to his desk and showed me a 360 degree photo of the charred casino. I pointed out the burned craps table that I had taken some melted dice and a charred silver dollar from the night of the fire.

I explained that I had just bought a house and would like to stay in Las Vegas, but they said, "If you get hired by us that ain't happening."

Just like that I said, "Then I'll move."

John just smiled and said to Mike, "I like this kid!"

Mike then got up and called the big boss, Walt, in San Francisco. I was asked if I would fly to San Francisco on my own dime for an interview. I said, "Of course."

I had never been to San Francisco before, but all I needed was a date, time, address, and the name of the person I needed to see.

I never told anyone about what I was doing. I flew to San Francisco in my three piece grey suit with grey patent leather pointy shoes. I got into the cab and said, "525 Market Street...downtown."

The city was beautiful; there were flowers everywhere, the sun was shining, and it was clear and crisp. I got there a half hour early.

This time I was all dressed up and had my game face on. I wanted to be a Special Agent with ATF!

I got to the 34th floor and it was a nice big office. I asked to see Mr. Wysocki and explained I was a little early for a 1 p.m. appointment. "I was sent from your Las Vegas office for an interview," I explained.

She asked me to be seated, so I sat. There was a Police Chief magazine on the table, so I took a look at it never knowing that in a couple hours my life would be changed for good!

Thank God ATF was hiring and that would hopefully be my ticket out of Sin City!

Epilogue

I loved being a Las Vegas cop! Truth be known, it was a fraternity like no other. It would always amaze me to see the helter-skelter of the officers when one of their own was in trouble or when shots were fired. "444" was the magic call sign that meant "all hell is breaking loose" because one of our own is in trouble or down. All other calls for duty paled in comparison. In other words…It was show time, baby!

In reality it was a beautiful thing to witness and be a part of. Adrenaline pumping, lights flashing, sirens blaring from all over town. You could feel it in the air. You just knew someone was going down!

This is exactly why first responders are all heroes. The bell rings and they come running. They run to trouble while others run away! It is such a noble profession and cops and firemen are a special breed of cat.

That is why it pains me to this day to see Monday morning quarterbacks who never put on a uniform and tried to make an arrest of someone who hated them and didn't want to go to jail. They are quick to judge and critique, but in reality, they are talking out of their collective asses. They always say the suspect was "unarmed". If you are trying to put someone in handcuffs and they are resisting what do you think happens when they are stronger than you and you lose the fight? How long do you think they will remain "unarmed" if they win the fight?

In my case, even though I loved the job in Las Vegas, I became somewhat bitter but mostly hurt about the way I was treated by my own people. I started to feel my number might be up. I mean, they had me take a polygraph test, they frowned on my interest in sending a snitch into Caesar's Palace to clean up their security scam, and they attempted to set me up on a traffic stop. All this weighed heavily on me, and I was beginning to not love the job like before. It was sad because it was my own people causing me the pain. I moved there from Chicago to follow my law enforcement dream and they had the nerve to try and set me up? Then one summer day in 1983, God shed some light on me and my predicament as the Feds and ATF were hiring again!

When I had the opportunity to go and be a Federal Agent I jumped at the chance. Ever since my junior year in college I had heard that ATF was the way to go. The summer of 1983, they started hiring again so I opted for greener pastures and a Federal badge. I knew it was a better retirement and my ticket to possibly get back to Chicago, my home town.

I guess it was also time to hang up the old METRO uniform, so to speak. As luck would have it things all worked out and I eventually retired from my Special Agent position with ATF and Federal service 24 years later in 2007.

The few things that soured me in Las Vegas do not detract from the fun I had there, the experience I gained, and the friends I made. Las Vegas METRO is a great police department!

After leaving Las Vegas I went on to become a Special Agent with ATF in San Francisco, where I worked in the Organized Crime Drug Enforcement Task Force. My travels over the next 24 years as a Fed were various and challenging. I worked in San Francisco, New York City, Albuquerque, Philadelphia, Washington DC, Chicago, and Tucson. I was also assigned to the white house as the ATF Representative to the Drug Czar's office and actually briefed President Clinton in 1993 regarding the families of the slain ATF Agents at Waco. I retired from Federal service in 2007 and currently reside in Tucson with my lovely wife Marcie and two cats, Princess and Tigger.

Deep Thoughts: Very Simple...Respect and Comply!

You know what pisses me off? It's all these non-law enforcement "Monday morning quarterback" types attempting to critique and opine about officer involved shootings. That is as crazy as me trying to explain brain surgery to you without ever going to Medical school or conducting a single operation!

I have been involved in police shootings and have also investigated a few during my nearly 30 year law enforcement career. I can tell you that it is always shocking to witness somebody getting shot. It is equally as shocking to see it over and over again on a video recording. It is far more horrific to witness it in person.

I must caution you, though, that whatever you see is not the entire story. If you are black and you see a white cop shoot a black person, you assume it was racially motivated. You usually have no clue as to what caused the situation, but all you see is a violent act against one of your own. It is often natural to opine the poor black guy was shot by the white racist cop for no other reason other than he is black. Natural perhaps, but wrong, and here is why...

A few years ago in Ferguson, Missouri, a white police officer shot and killed a black man. It was incorrectly purported that the man had his hands up and was shot "execution style" in the back. That never happened! Eyewitnesses originally lied. The DOJ sent 40 FBI Agents to investigate possible civil rights violations. In the end, the shooting was justified, witnesses recanted, and the FBI found no violations. Unfortunately for the white officer, he had to resign (for safety reasons) and leave town.

So let this be a lesson to us all...In any police shooting we have no idea initially why officers were dispatched to the scene. We have no idea if the suspect was drugged out of their mind, had a gun or knife in his or her pocket, had a felony warrant for his or her arrest, or matched the description of an armed robbery suspect.

However, if you look closely at police shootings, when they happen the subject (no matter what color they are or what color the cop is) failed to comply and/or resisted arrest. This, I assure you, is the problem in 99% of all police shootings against "unarmed" subjects.

No subject is ever "unarmed" if they choose to get into a physical altercation with an officer. This is because if the officer loses the fight, they will most likely lose their gun and possibly their life. So please keep that in mind! It really doesn't matter what color the cop is or the subject is; when you fail to comply or grab for an officer's gun, you will have a problem and could get shot.

So please, no matter who your parents are, if you are stopped by police, be respectful and follow all police commands. For that short moment in your life they are "in charge" whether you like it or not. If an officer tells you to drop it, drop it! If they tell you to stop, stop! Know that police officers are on high alert in today's world when people shoot cops just because they are cops. They are targets and still put their lives on the line to protect strangers like us. Isn't that worth something?

Even if you hate cops and you are the biggest racist on the planet, please just pretend to be respectful and comply with all commands, and I assure you there will be no problems. If you don't believe me, take the time to objectively review each shooting situation and you will see that aggression and non-compliance causes the problems.

Lastly, when an officer stops a car they often times have no clue as to the color or gender of the occupants. The same thing goes on a dispatched call. Do you actually think that a cop cares what color you are when you are resisting arrest? Do you think that if a black guy gets to a weapon he can do more damage than a white guy or Hispanic guy? Why do you think on a traffic stop the officers never want the subject to go back to their car? Trust me, all cops want to do is go home that night. You should just focus on following lawful commands. Period.

Finally, I don't care how many BLM T-shirts are printed, how many times it is painted in the streets or how many athletes take a knee during our National Anthem. If you fail to follow lawful police commands, no matter what color you are, you will have problems. So please, respect and comply and it will be a safer America for all.

And if a cop ever does you wrong, get his or her name and get yourself a good lawyer. Every city has deep pockets.

Please be smart...think survival!

Thank you, be safe and God bless America!

JUSTICE FOR DALLAS

Retired Special Agent, Mark Rusin, Turns Shocking & Brutal Real-World Murder Case into Compelling New Novel

Written by Mark Rusin and based on the most intricate and emotional murder case of his three-decade career in law enforcement, 'Justice for Dallas' takes readers back to 1986 as an entire family is slain. Embroiling the reader in the worlds of drugs, motorcycle gangs and good old-fashioned detective work, Rusin's novel offers an insight into an unbelievable reality that actually does exist.

Tucson, AZ – During his thirty-plus years as a law enforcement officer, Mark Rusin experienced the thick and thin of life as a Las Vegas cop. From pulling bodies out of the 1980 MGM Grand Hotel fire to numerous exciting undercover cases, one out-of-the-blue murder investigation during his tenure with the Federal Bureau of Alcohol, Tobacco, Firearms & Explosives (ATF) was so impactful that the now-retired Rusin is turning it into a powerful new novel.

'Justice for Dallas' straddles fact and fiction to take readers into the investigation of a quadruple murder that left the ATF dumbfounded. While many confidential aspects of the case have been changed within the book, the crime's premise, circumstances and conclusions remain as haunting and chilling as when Rusin first took on the case.

Synopsis:

As a rookie ATF Agent, Marko Novak is assigned one of the most brutal murder investigations in northern California history. A mother, father, and 15-year old son are all shot "execution style" and their 5-year old daughter, Dallas has her throat slit from ear to ear. Their house is then doused in kerosene and set ablaze in an effort for the murderers to cover their tracks. Marko vows to find the killer(s) as he is emotionally affected by the crime scene photos, especially by the way the little girl died.

The investigation takes the reader on a wild ride to find the truth as the author Mark Rusin attempts to 'bring them along' on this investigative journey. The lives of outlaw motorcycle gangs are exposed along with the Federal bureaucracy as witness intimidation is dealt with, along with a host of other obstacles that need to be overcome in an effort to finally find truth and justice. *One pristine bullet, a motorcycle, some rug soaked in kerosene and 4 dead bodies are all the investigators had to go on from the crime scene. Later, a drug deal gone bad and some good old fashioned police work help make the case come together, but would it be enough?*

"Most authors construct narratives in their heads – but I've walked, smelt and touched this scene in real-life," says Rusin, who collaborated with Priscilla Barton during the book's composition. "This allows me to take readers to a level of depth that is unmatched in other books."

Continuing, "I suppose it could be classed as 'faction'; as the only changes I have made are to preserve some of the case's more sensitive aspects. Aside from that, everything is frighteningly close to reality. Believe me, this was one emotional case and it still haunts me today. I hope it gives readers plenty to think about."

To date the novel has garnered rave reviews. For example, Cynthia Koss comments, "'Justice for Dallas' is quite captivating, especially since this book is about a real case. Mark Rusin shows the human side of an actual investigation where innocent people lost their lives. It is a fast paced, easy to read book and I couldn't put it down."

Mike Witzgall offered his praise, "As only a fellow cop could write. Justice for Dallas is authentic and riveting."

Max T. adds, "Wow, what a thriller. Caution: Once you start this book, there's no putting it down. This was obviously written by a cop - because it has a believability that is hard to beat. It was riveting. When do we get more from Mr. Rusin?!"

'Justice for Dallas' is available now: http://amzn.to/1i5yJBH. For more information, visit the author's official website: http://www.markrusin.com.

About the Author

MARK RUSIN was born and raised on the south side of Chicago where he attended first Our Lady of the Snows Grammar School and then Quigley South High School. He went on to Western Illinois University graduating in 1977 with a Bachelor of Science Degree in Law Enforcement Administration.

From a young age, Mark dreamed first about playing professional hockey for his hometown Blackhawks and second about being a cop.

His second dream came true when on January 16, 1980 he was sworn in as a Las Vegas Metropolitan Police Officer. There he gained his street Masters Degree over the next four years and his most memorable police calls and stories are contained in this book: ***METRO: Sin City Chronicles***. His first published article appeared in the 2005 Las Vegas Review Journal regarding the 25th anniversary of the MGM Grand Hotel fire in November, 1980. Mark who was a rookie officer at that time was assigned to pull dead bodies from the hotel.

Mark left the Las Vegas Metro Police Force in December 1983 for "greener pastures" and a Federal Badge with the Bureau of Alcohol, Tobacco, Firearms and Explosives (ATF.)

Over the next 24 years his assignments as an ATF Special Agent took him on a wild ride that included:

- The Organized Crime Drug Enforcement Task Force in San Francisco where he worked on one of the most brutal quadruple homicides involving the most notorious motorcycle gang: The Hells Angels.
- See his October 2013 published book ***Justice For Dallas***
- Washington, DC and ATF's arson and explosives division where he monitored major arson fires and bombings across the US.
- New York City, where in 1989 he helped establish the Jamaican Posse Task Force (due to the significant number of drug and gang related murders that year in Manhattan.)
- Albuquerque, New Mexico where he ran the criminal enforcement group there in 1990.
- Philadelphia, Pennsylvania where he supervised the criminal enforcement group responsible for the biggest cocaine bust in that city's history.
- Washington, DC where he ran the ATF International Alcohol and Tobacco Interdiction unit. In 1993 Mark was assigned to brief President Bill Clinton on the slain ATF special agents and their families regarding the shootout at the Branch Davidian Compound in Waco, Texas.
- Chicago, Illinois where he was the ATF Assistant Special Agent in Charge and supervised enforcement operations there for the state of Illinois. While at that post, Mark earned the State of Illinois' Law Enforcement Officer of the Year Award for 1997-1998.

- Washington, DC where he was ATF's representative at the White House for both the Clinton and Bush Administrations.
- From 1999-2003 Mark was assigned to the Executive Office of the President as an advisor to the Nation's Drug Czar.
- Tucson, Arizona where he was the western regional coordinator for ATF's Ballistic Imaging Program.
- Mark also protected all US Presidents from 1983-2003 (Ronald Reagan through George W. Bush.)

Mark retired from Federal Service in March 2007 and currently resides in Tucson, Arizona. He spends his time writing, golfing and still dreaming about some day playing for his Chicago Blackhawks.

Rose Garden — May, 1993

NEVER FORGET!

These four ATF Special Agents gave the ultimate sacrifice in Waco, Texas on February 28, 1993. We will "Never Forget" them and their families!

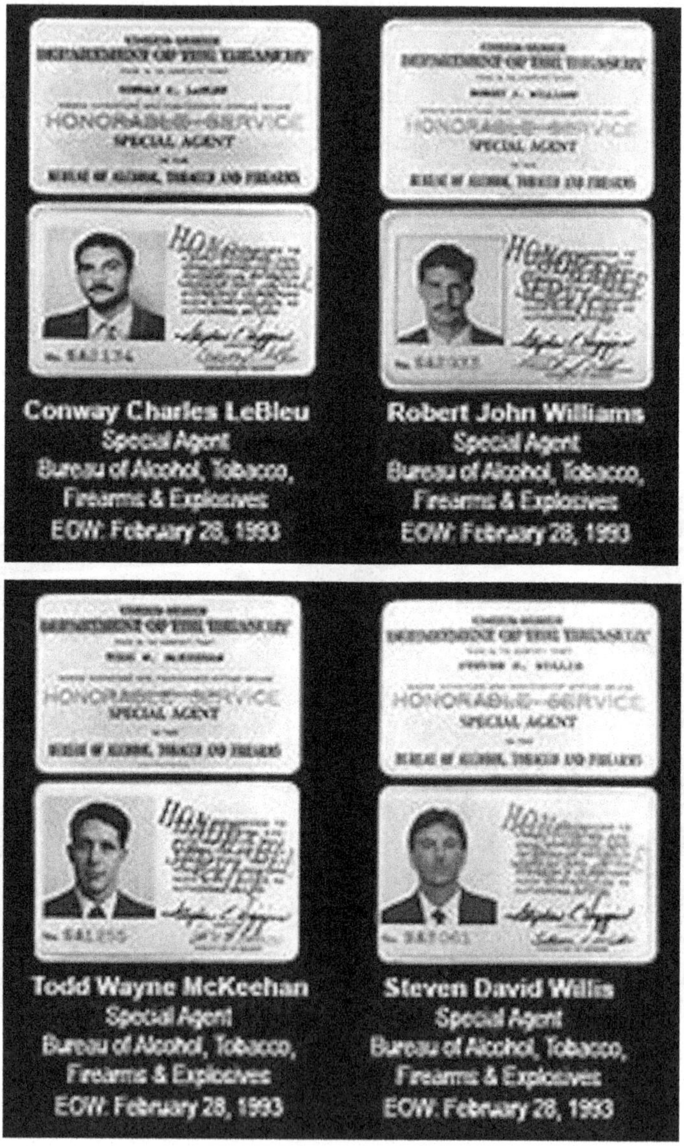

Made in the USA
Las Vegas, NV
14 January 2021

15800793R00100